Editor
Cynthia Davidson

Section Guest Editor
Jaime Solares Carmona

Managing Editor
Patrick Templeton

Editorial Intern
Motuma Tulu

Protagonists
Thomas Daniell
Todd Gannon
Catherine Ingraham
Sanford Kwinter
Manuel Orazi
Bryony Roberts
Julie Rose
Sarah Whiting

What does it mean to read today? When I open my digital subscription to the *New York Times*, if the "headline" isn't enough bait to warrant a click, the "read time" might be. Today, for example, the lead story is labeled a "3 MIN READ."

Three minutes. One hundred eighty seconds. Sounds more like a rate of consumption than reading. Yet I admit to looking for the read time lately and choosing a story to match the length of a subway ride or the wait in the lunch line at Sweetgreen.

Similarly, I find myself impatient with Instagram stories (my only social media vice). It may be the incessant proliferation of advertising that causes me to swipe faster and faster, or because I seldom see posts by actual friends. And it rarely involves reading.

Earlier this year I met a former *Bloomberg News* editor who told me that the best writing today is one-sentence paragraphs. Not only because they're a faster read but also – and he demonstrated this – because they're the best format for reading on a phone.

That phone, of course, is the new "machine for living." *Log*, on the other hand, is a machine for reading – to riff on French poet Paul Valéry's statement that "a book is a machine for reading."

When I googled Valéry to fact-check my memory, an unsolicited AI Overview at the top of the screen summed up Valéry's use of the phrase: "to describe how a book is not just a passive object, but an actively constructed experience in the mind of the reader . . . that generates meaning through its structure and language."

Structure and language also have multiple meanings in architecture. Not just for reading words but for reading plans, sections, axonometrics, Rhino models, and buildings themselves: proportion, style, symbolism… And all of that working of the mind takes time.

I've often said that I believe in the slow space of the page – not the webpage but the printed page. I feel the difference when I move from my weekday online *New York Times* to the weekend print editions. I can spend hours paging through the paper on a Sunday and reading surprising stories, especially in the Real Estate and Metropolitan sections, and it doesn't feel like consumption (usually I'm consuming a chocolate-ginger scone with a café au lait). It feels like an "actively constructed experience" in my mind. The space and time for thoughtfulness.

Of course, ultimately, it's the thoughtfulness of others – the writers – who make reading possible. Who make this issue of *Log*, which includes our first long look at South American architecture and criticism, thanks to guest editor Jaime Solares Carmona, possible. So make yourself an espresso – with coffee beans from south of the equator – and rediscover what it can mean to take the time to read today, especially to read about architecture. – *CD*

www.anycorp.com

Log

Fall 2024   Observations on architecture and the contemporary city

e-flux Index

www.e-flux.com/index

REFLECTIONS ON ARCHITECTURE

From Park Books
Meditations in Entropy
The Work of Kashef Chowdhury / URBANA
in Bangladesh
Kashef Chowdhury, et al.

This book documents the innovative work of the
Dhaka-based practice Kashef Chowdhury / URBANA
as it adapts to the reality of climate change.
Cloth $65.00

From Scheidegger & Spiess
Hans Pieler
Architectures of Time
**Edited by Hubertus von Amelunxen and
Ali Ghandtschi**
Photography by Hans Pieler

Lavishly illustrated and featuring illuminating essays,
the first-ever book on Hans Pieler's photographs of
calendar buildings.
Cloth $65.00

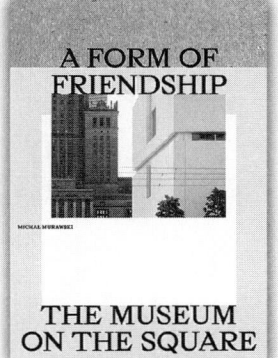

From the Museum of Modern Art in Warsaw
A Form of Friendship
The Museum on the Square
Michal Murawski

A subjective, candid, multi-vocal story about the creation of
the building of the Museum of Modern Art in Warsaw.
Paper $35.00

From Hirmer Publishers
The Library
An Open Book
Edited by Ido Bruno and Yad Hanadiv

This book takes the reader on a journey that transcends
stone and mortar to explore the importance of libraries in
our fast-paced digital age. The book features original short
stories, paintings, photographs, and comics by some of the
world's leading authors and artists.
Cloth $60.00

Distributed by the University of Chicago Press
www.press.uchicago.edu

Architecture and Human Spaces

From CHICAGO
Window Shopping with Helen Keller
Architecture and Disability in Modern Culture
David Serlin
"*Window Shopping with Helen Keller* weaves together a remarkably diverse range of biographies, sites, and concepts. Serlin demonstrates that the disabled reimagining of buildings and cities extends far beyond, and well before, the arrival of 'accessible architecture.'"—David Gissen, The New School
Paper $30.00

Building the Metropolis
Architecture, Construction, and Labor in New York City, 1880–1935
Alexander Wood
"Wood shifts the lens of the typical architectural and urban history away from the architect and toward the construction industry and, significantly, the workers themselves."—Gail Fenske, author of *The Skyscraper and the City*
Cloth $35.00

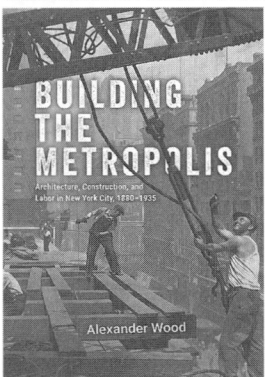

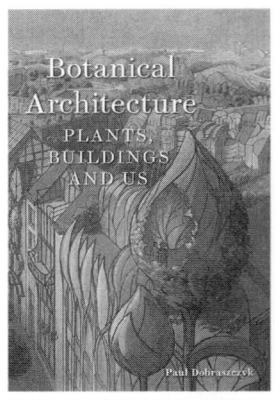

From 🕷 **Reaktion**
Botanical Architecture
Plants, Buildings and Us
Paul Dobraszczyk
"Focusing by turns on seeds, roots, trunks, branches, leaves, flowers, canopies, and vegetal communities that include all living beings, *Botanical Architecture* is a *tour d'imagination* of thinking with plants."—Michael Marder, author of *Time is a Plant*
Cloth $35.00

Playgrounds
The Experimental Years
Ben Highmore
"Highmore shares an exquisitely written, hopeful narrative on the innovative qualities and progressive principals found in the post-war urban experimental playground movement."—Raiford Guins, Indiana University
Cloth $35.00

The University of Chicago Press www.press.uchicago.edu

TO BUILD LAW

Berlin   b+

CO2

38%

CO2 emissions of building sector versus 8% transportation sector

Source: European Environment Agency (https://www.eea.europa.eu/ims/greenhouse-gas-emissions-from-energy)

11.12.2024 – 25.5.2025

GROUNDWORK

TO BUILD LAW, THE SECOND CHAPTER OF GROUNDWORK, CLOSELY OBSERVES THE BPLUS.XYZ (B+) TEAM DURING THE DEVELOPMENT OF A EUROPEAN CITIZENS' INITIATIVE TO CAMPAIGN FOR A SYSTEMIC SHIFT IN THE WAY WE VALUE OUR BUILT ENVIRONMENT.

CCA

cca.qc.ca/groundwork

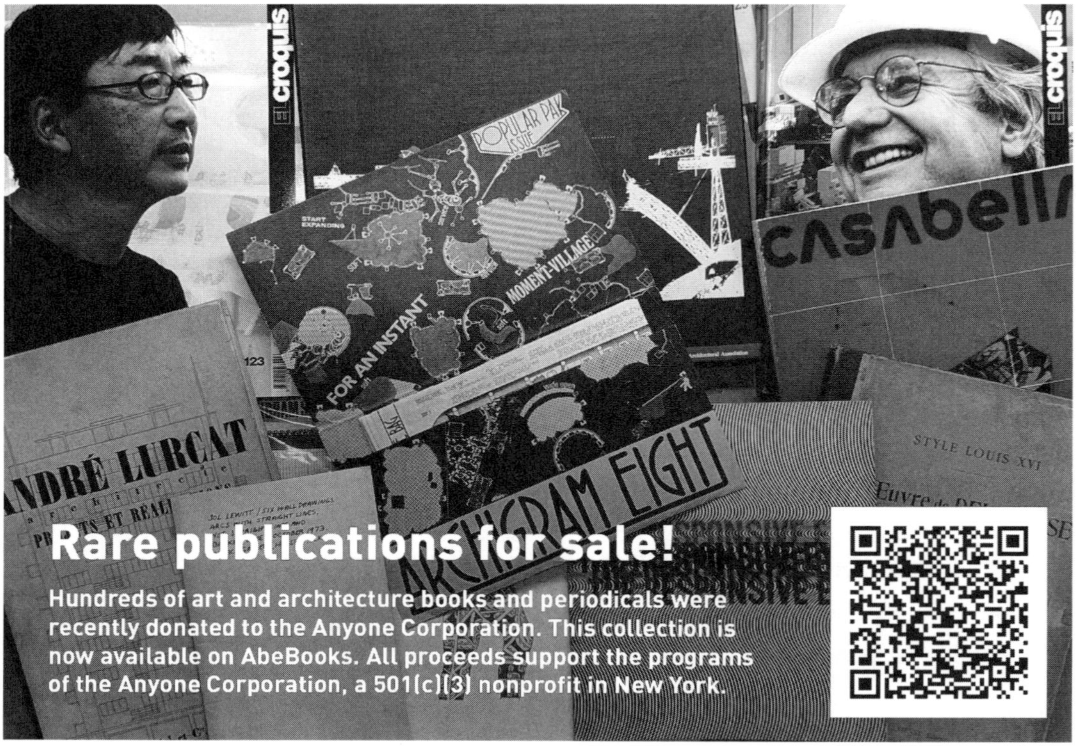

Architecture *From*  PARK BOOKS

Arata Isozaki
In Formation
Edited by Xiangning Li
Arata Isozaki is the first new work on the architect in fifteen years.
Conceived in collaboration with Arata Isozaki & Associates,
it features photographs, plans, model images, drawings, and
watercolors from all periods of Isozaki's career.
PAPER $65.00

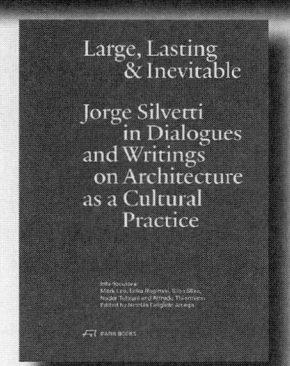

Large, Lasting & Inevitable
*Jorge Silvetti in Dialogues and Writings on Architecture as a
Cultural Practice*
Jorge Silvetti
Edited by Nicolás Delgado Alcega
Large, Lasting & Inevitable is a reflection on Jorge Silvetti's five decades
in architecture, set against the backdrop of fervent discussions about
discourse, history, cultural politics, and practice today.
PAPER $40.00

Driftin g Symmetries
*Projects, Provocations, and other Enduring Models by Weiss/
Manfredi*
Marion Weiss and Michael Manfredi
Edited by Eric Bellin
Featuring Weiss/Manfredi's most acclaimed built works, *Drifting
Symmetries* is a manual for expanding the terrain of contemporary
architecture to construct more resilient settings for contemporary life.
CLOTH $65.00

Modern Buildings in Blackheath and Greenwich
London 1950–2000
Ana Francisco Sutherland
A tribute and guide to modern housing architecture in post-WWII
London, *Modern Buildings in Blackheath and Greenwich* also takes a
broader look at the evolution of modern English architecture in the
context of social and housing policies of the time.
CLOTH $45.00

Distributed by the University of Chicago Press www.press.uchicago.edu

After the Anybody conference in Buenos Aires, in 1996, the participants and friends visited Le Corbusier's Dr. Curutchet House in La Plata. In a group photo in front of the house, Fred Jameson, tall and dressed in white, stands beside his friend, cultural critic Masao Miyoshi, who wears black. © Anyone Corporation fonds, Canadian Centre for Architecture, Montreal.

Michael Speaks

Fredric Jameson: The End of an Era

Recently I began reading Fredric Jameson's *The Years of Theory* (2024), an account of postwar French thought he originally delivered as an online seminar during the pandemic and published shortly after his death on September 22, at the age of 90. It is now Jameson's last book, and it returns him full circle to his own intellectual beginnings, to Sartre, the philosopher, novelist, and playwright who – in Jameson's admittedly idiosyncratic account – set the stage and provided the example for the transition from academic philosophy to "theory" and for a new kind of intellectual practice freed from disciplinary obligations and conventions. It was a path, Jameson argues, taken by nearly all the major French theorists, and one that suited Jameson well, leading him to write countless essays and books on an impossibly wide range of topics, from literature to film and to architecture.

Jameson wrote many essays on architecture and used architecture in his most well-known book, *Postmodernism, or, the Cultural Logic of Late Capitalism* (1991), to argue for postmodernism as a historical period rather than as a style. For Jameson, architecture was a "privileged" subject, as he often remarked, because it offered clues to the emergence of a new kind of late capitalist space, or hyperspace, as he called it. It also offered clues to analyze and understand those spaces, as he showed in his reading of the work of Frank Gehry and John Portman. Architecture is also, of all cultural forms, the most connected to the economic base, and thus offers the most tangible evidence for the kind of Marxian analysis that defines his work. And, as Jameson revealed in "Architecture and the Critique of Ideology," his brilliant essay on Manfredo Tafuri's *Architecture and Utopia* (1973), architecture is also a superstructural concern, one implicated in ideology and the limits of utopia and utopian or class-based architecture.

But Jameson's most sustained focus on architecture came in the essays he wrote for the Any Conference books published from 1992 to 2001 by the Anyone Corporation. Indeed, any analysis of Jameson's focus on architecture must necessarily take these essays into account not only because of their content but also because of their consistency, one each year,

Fredric Jameson, *The Years of Theory: Postwar French Thought to the Present.* Verso, 2024. 458 pages.

and because of their global orientation, written, as they were, to focus on 10 urban locales around the world. Produced from a series of 10 conferences – Anyone, Anywhere, Anyway, Anyplace, etc. – each held in a different location – Los Angeles, Yufuin, Barcelona, Montreal, etc. – all of which Jameson attended, these books now document an important historical period in which theory of the kind Jameson distinguishes from philosophy, and of which his work was an example, became the intellectual dominant of architecture discourse, especially in the architecture academy, and especially in the United States, the capital of architecture theory during the 1990s.

In *The Years of Theory,* Jameson proposes that French theory emerged with the break that thinkers like Gilles Deleuze, Jacques Lacan, Michel Foucault, and others made with Sartre's systemic approach to philosophy: "I think the passage from philosophy to what we call 'theory' is part of that liberation. Suddenly, philosophy is freed from its systemic ambitions." Systemic philosophy, and especially phenomenology, was abandoned in favor of new "reading" practices enabled by structural linguistics, like those employed by Louis Althusser in *Reading Capital* (1965) and Roland Barthes in *S/Z* (1970). Sartre opened the door for "writing philosophy in a new way," Jameson asserts, and these French thinkers walked through it to the freedom of a new philosophical practice he calls theory. When the work and reading protocols of these and other French thinkers were introduced into the American academy, however, mostly through comparative literature programs like those in which Jameson spent his career, they were removed from the philosophical and political contexts in which they had been produced, and soon became the foundation for practices and products more autonomous, abstract, and commodified than the French theory practiced and produced in France. This new, "Americanized" theory broke entirely with the still philosophical ambitions of French theory and emerged, fully formed, in the mid-1980s, with adherents in nearly every discipline, including architecture. Bookstores created special theory sections as if it were a new discipline and often organized tables on which to display the new "theory" books. New comparative literature programs such as the one at UC Irvine, where Jacques Derrida taught, and the literature program at Duke University, which Jameson founded and where he taught until his death, were created, seemingly devoid of disciplinary specificity, to study, produce, and teach theory.

This Americanized theory was introduced into the architecture academy largely through Peter Eisenman's Institute for Architecture and Urban Studies, and through its journal *Oppositions*. *Assemblage*, edited by K. Michael Hays and Alicia Kennedy, also played a role in the development and dissemination of architecture theory in the American academy, while Hays's definitive anthology, *Architecture Theory since 1968* (2000), which collected and codified the work of the major theorists, served as architecture theory's summative, closing act, defining, as do all anthologies, architecture theory as a historical rather than contemporary concern. While Jameson refers to theory as the reading practice that replaced systemic philosophy, the "years of theory" in architecture were by contrast an American affair in which architecture theory became the practice, product, and intellectual dominant of the American architecture academy beginning in the mid-1980s and ending just after the turn of the century and millenium. These were also, uncoincidentally, the peak years of American-led globalization and the years in which architecture – especially the Any-affiliated avant-garde – exercised its greatest cultural and intellectual influence.

Any is also the literal and discursive portal through which I and a number of theory-trained academics entered this very specialized architecture discourse in the 1990s. I was a dissertation student at Duke, studying with Jameson. I had published a few essays on architecture in European newspapers and an interview with Jameson in *Assemblage* when I attended, with Jameson, the Anywhere conference in Yufuin, Japan, in the late spring of 1992. It was a gathering of the most important architecture and intellectual figures from the period, including Arata Isozaki, Tadao Ando, Toyo Ito, Kojin Karatani, Shigehiko Hasumi, Elizabeth Diller, Peter Eisenman, Rem Koolhaas, Phyllis Lambert, etc. The conference was held in a small train station designed by Isozaki and broadcast live to an auditorium in Tokyo. Among my most vivid memories of that trip and event are the long, impromptu conversation I had with Derrida on the roof deck of the overnight ferry we took across the Inland Sea, during which he admitted that he was most looking forward to the hot springs in Yufuin (not as much the architecture and philosophy discussion); the strange circumstance of Jameson "translating" Derrida's lecture from French to English as the resident translators could not follow the complexities of Derrida's speech, read, of course, from a written text; the visit to the Nexus World development in Fukuoka, master planned by Isozaki; and the tour Koolhaas led through his housing project there, still among my favorite OMA buildings. I also spent time with and stayed at the home of Karatani, whose Writing Architecture Series book, *Architecture as Metaphor* (1995), I later edited with translator Sabu Kohso.

Back in Durham, I had several conversations with Jameson about the conference, and later that summer, I joined the Anyone Corporation as senior editor of *ANY Magazine* and subsequently helped launch the Writing Architecture Series. I attended two more Any conferences – Barcelona and Montreal – and spent time at each with Jameson, catching up and discussing his views on the conference and the assembled speakers. On one occasion, in Barcelona, Jameson wanted to search for a restaurant he had visited many years prior, when he was a student traveling in Europe, and while we were searching, we encountered one of the conference speakers, André Glucksmann, a former member of the Nouveaux Philosophes, the group of French intellectuals who in the 1970s launched a harsh critique of Marxism. Jameson was appalled that Glucksmann, an avowed post- (or anti-) Marxist, had been invited and said as much before we quickly crossed the street to find, by chance, the very restaurant for which we had been searching.

Jameson begins *The Years of Theory* with Sartre and breezes through a staggering number of thinkers, movements, and asides – though not enough gossip – before concluding with Quentin Meillassoux, the most important member in the last school of French thought – Speculative Realism – to gain any (though not much) traction in the architecture academy. While the book itself charts the transition from philosophy to theory, its publication this fall and the near simultaneous passing of Jameson marks a different kind of transition than the one documented therein. In my view, it marks the end of an era. In a series of articles and essays published in the early 2000s, I argued that theory, especially architecture theory, had lost touch with the contemporary world, and especially with architecture practice, which for some time had begun to conform to a new intellectual dominant: intelligence. Intelligence, I argued, was a provisional, post-Enlightenment form of knowledge produced and used by practitioners rather than a preexisting philosophical truth or theoretical ideology that motivated or guided design and practice. I do not want to rehearse too much of that argument here but merely to insist that while this new intellectual dominant – intelligence – superseded and made irrelevant

theory, which had previously superseded and made irrelevant philosophy, the argument for the emergence of a
new intellectual dominant was consistent with, rather than
oppositional to – as many suggested at the time – Jameson's
periodizing approach. Indeed, I was simply extending his
periodizing argument beyond theory to argue for a new
intellectual dominant. Though I never discussed this with
Jameson, I am sure he would have agreed.

What, then, does Jameson's passing mark? What era is
over, specifically in architecture? Before answering, it is first
important to observe that what is *not* over and what has not
disappeared with his passing is architecture ideology and the
intellectual dominant within which it was produced: theory.
And that is because architecture ideology and theory were
already exhausted by the time of the last Any conference
in New York in 2000, already before the last issues of *ANY
Magazine* and *Assemblage* were published. No, those concerns have long disappeared from architecture discourse
along with their philosophical, Enlightenment antecedents.
Log, the magazine in which I write these words, and the most
recent Anyone Corporation publication, is a wonderful contemporary exploration of architectural thought and reflection, but it is decidedly not philosophical-truth asserting or
theoretical-ideological advocating. It is, like all architecture intellectual production today, including and especially
nearly everything produced in the architecture academy,
post-Enlightenment: provocative, eclectic, myopic, interesting, stimulating, and without singular purpose or direction.
Log, I would argue, is a journal of architectural intelligence,
and as such is the most representative and important publication of contemporary architecture thinking and discourse.
No, what has ended with Jameson's passing is the *motivation*

to historicize, or periodize, as he called it, with the *purpose* of discovering the stable, historical ground or conceptual space from which to launch any counter-ideology, theory, or critique. The point of periodizing and, indeed, of cognitive mapping – Jameson's call for an aesthetic practice that could provide the necessary "critical distance" to map the global capitalist system – which are his two greatest gifts to architecture discourse, is that they are meant to leverage the ground and space necessary for the establishment of any new philosophical truth or theoretical ideology. That era – of philosophy and theory and the search for new tools and strategies to continue the Enlightenment project – is now over. Periodizing, of the kind I engaged when I asserted the emergence of intelligence, obviously continues, but what is lost, what has forever disappeared, is the motivation and ambition to periodize or cognitively map with a view to establishing a new architecture philosophical truth or theoretical ideology. We can be thankful or nostalgic about that, but it is simply a fact. What we can all be grateful for, however, is the life and work of Fredric Jameson. I will always be a fellow traveler.

Michael Speaks is dean and professor at the Syracuse University School of Architecture. Previously, he was dean and professor at the University of Kentucky College of Design from 2008–13, and director of the graduate program and founding director of the Metropolitan Research and Design postgraduate program at SCI-Arc from 1998–2008.

Fernanda Canales

Less Is Incomplete

Mies van der Rohe said "Less is more" to defend simplicity in architecture, but that very simplicity led architectural practice to fall short, to always be incomplete. After "Less is more" came "Less is a bore," Robert Venturi's statement against the repetition of the simple forms of the Modern Movement, which opened the door to shamelessly combining styles during 1980s postmodernism. Then came "Less is just less," used by Pier Vittorio Aureli to denounce the false austerity of minimalism associated with consumer capitalism at the beginning of the 21st century. Against the architecture of neoliberalism, which amplified inequalities, Aureli proposed that "Less is enough" in a call to reduce the accumulation of possessions and explore the advantages of sharing. These four principles – less is more, less is a bore, less is less, and less is enough – explain the architecture of the past 100 years, but more important, they also reveal the narrowness of the visions on which we have built our world.

Architecture is mainly focused on the production of buildings conceived as isolated objects, but the 21st century demands new thinking based on coexistence. Today, it is difficult to explain Mies's dictum when we know that the bronze I-beams on the facades of his Seagram Building in New York were used only for decorative purposes. Measuring 515 feet long, the I-beams made Seagram the most expensive skyscraper in the world for decades. It is also notable that boredom in architecture was not eliminated by the unconstrained formal repertoire of postmodernism. The aim for less is not only a bore, as Venturi claimed, but also simply less, as Aureli states, yet, for many it will never be enough.

Since the Industrial Revolution, architecture has contributed to a world based on a notion of productivity, a world designed to provide maximum benefits for a select few while ignoring the destructive consequences that come with one-sided views of progress. The ethos of universal efficiency does not ask, Efficient for whom and at what cost? The concept of profit varies depending on the definition of benefit: long- or short-term, individual or collective. Unlike most 20th-century architects, Aureli defends moderation instead of abundance, habitability versus production, and coexistence over supremacy, inspiring new ways of life based on reciprocity. His dictum revives Hannes Meyer's lessons from the 1920s in an attempt to solve the minimum for individual life while obtaining maximum advantages for the collective. Aureli stands against both the premise of growth for the sake of growth and the rhetoric of scarcity. However, it is not enough simply to search for a balanced distribution of wealth; the future of humankind lies in the inclusion of all entities. We need to stop building a world that disregards living entities that do not have a voice and recognize that we have not done enough to include everyone and everything that has been systematically neglected. To change architecture, to stop it from being one of the most destructive industries on the planet, we need to acknowledge that less is incomplete.

The logic of less historically defended by architects is an insufficient concept because it does not represent everything that is alive, it is not caring, and its laws do not define the world. Architecture does not speak to everyone, nor does it allow everyone to speak. The values of the building industry are anchored in financial metrics elaborated by "specialists" for themselves. Frequently, the world is seen simply as property, with land in the service of profit-seeking owners but not necessarily under their care. But the world is not constructed only through buildings. Likewise, it is not based on binaries that divide everything into opposites: mine/yours, inside/outside, resource/waste, urban/rural, artificial/natural... leading to the gender, social, racial, and economic divisions that are so prominent. The widespread desire to dominate nature and colonize the world led humans to separate themselves from that world, threatening the basic principles of subsistence. Today, the future lies not in our control but in our dependencies. Human actions have created a geological force that places us in a new territory that we must understand differently. To go from building "on" the Earth to building "with" the Earth, we need not only to include opposing voices but also to listen to what has no voice.

Le Corbusier learned from ocean liners, Charlotte Perriand from common objects, Venturi and Denise Scott Brown from Las Vegas, and Jane Jacobs from the street. But until today, almost no attention has been paid to the ground on which we step. In just one cubic meter of land in the Southern Hemisphere there are around 50 spiders, 100 cockroaches, more than 100 worms, about 500 larvae, more than 50 thousand centipedes, 100 billion fungi, and

1. Francisco Díaz, *Suelo* (Talca, Chile: Editorial Bifurcaciones, Colección Perdidos en el Espacio, 2023), 23.

2. Dolores Hayden called them "material feminists" because, she wrote, "they dared to define a grand domestic revolution in women's material conditions." Dolores Hayden, *The Grand Domestic Revolution: A History of Feminist Designs for American Homes, Neighborhoods, and Cities* (Cambridge: MIT Press, 1982), 3.

about 10 billion bacteria.[1] But architects heard "fuck context" and obeyed.

When, almost 100 years ago, R. Buckminister Fuller described Earth as a spaceship that should work for everyone, it was still thought that humans were its most skilled operators. Today, however, there is a pressing need to reinvent our forms of interaction with the Earth, which has its own voice, by calling against the greed of the logic of more and the partiality of less. Instead of promoting a false idea of simplicity and conformance with less, can architecture create more complete forms of existence?

Architecture as Something Else

A more ample view of relations between living entities, buildings, and the environment emerged in the United States in the mid-19th and beginning of the 20th centuries, when Catharine Beecher, Ellen Henrietta Swallow Richards, Melusina Fay Peirce, Christine Frederick, Charlotte Perkins Gilman, Lillian Moller Gilbreth, and others, stood against the creation of a world divided into different spheres – public and private, living and working, etc. These writers, engineers, and activists, whose work started in the kitchen, developed an understanding of environmental systems. They considered space not as a realm inside a construction but as everything that comprises a place as a whole: activities, water, food, waste, time, and lives. For them, architecture was not simply a building but the main element in preventing illness, providing liberty, and saving national resources. For these domestic reformers, shaping a modern society meant a new concept of long-term efficiency and well-being for all people.

While these pioneer activists, known as the "material feminists," initiated a domestic revolution in women's material conditions, they were not interested in the material conditions of things but rather in their effects.[2] They were not a group, they were not all mothers or wives, and they had different views regarding the domestic sphere, female suffrage, religion, and gender roles. Their legacy was not simply the creation of feminist homes with socialized housework and childcare. Their work spanned nine decades, from 1840 to 1930, and led people to question the physical separation between the domestic and public spheres. These radical women were social and environmental reformers who fought, largely on their own and in unparalleled ways, to make architecture include more. For them, the term *domestic* did not describe the space inside a house but a local environment

Alice Constance Austin, "The General Plan of the Subdivision." Opposite page: "On a stream valley with blocks of houses." Both from *The Next Step: How to Plan for Beauty, Comfort, and Peace with Great Savings Effected by the Reduction of Waste*, 1935. Austin's proposals for ideal cities ensured that each unit is within a half-mile walk of civic centers. All images courtesy the author.

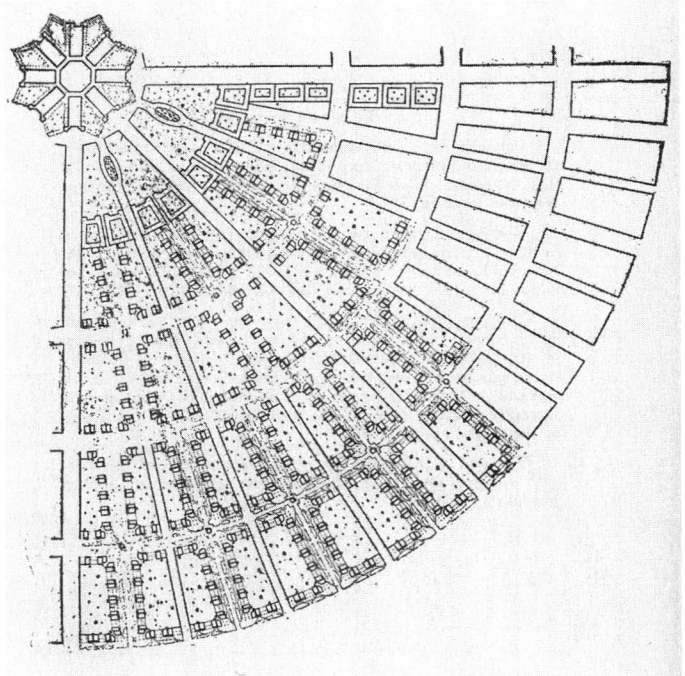

full of living beings with different needs. They were the first designers to understand the city as balanced environments, not as defined by the formal appearance of its architecture: its importance was not the buildings but the relations between them. They considered constructions as living organisms and parts of a broader system. They related spaces to labor and contemplated architecture as an adjustable ecosystem analogous to the skin of a body. From a kitchen designed to reduce the number of steps required to cook a meal, to a community that redefines the concepts of ownership and family, their contributions were also a battle against spaces that segregated human beings, especially unacknowledged populations.

These views were not due to a "natural" feminine condition but to hard-earned knowledge. Not a lady's instinct to "always look after little things," as was said at the time, but an effect produced by looking at things from the margins. Rather than a quality assigned to females at birth, theirs was a viewpoint that was more likely to develop if one had cooked 1,095 meals a year and then cleaned up afterward. Different questions are addressed and different solutions are reached if one spends life walking thousands of kilometers while carrying dishes or babies. According to philosopher Paulette Bernège, walking the eight meters that separated the kitchen counter from the dining table in her own apartment for 40

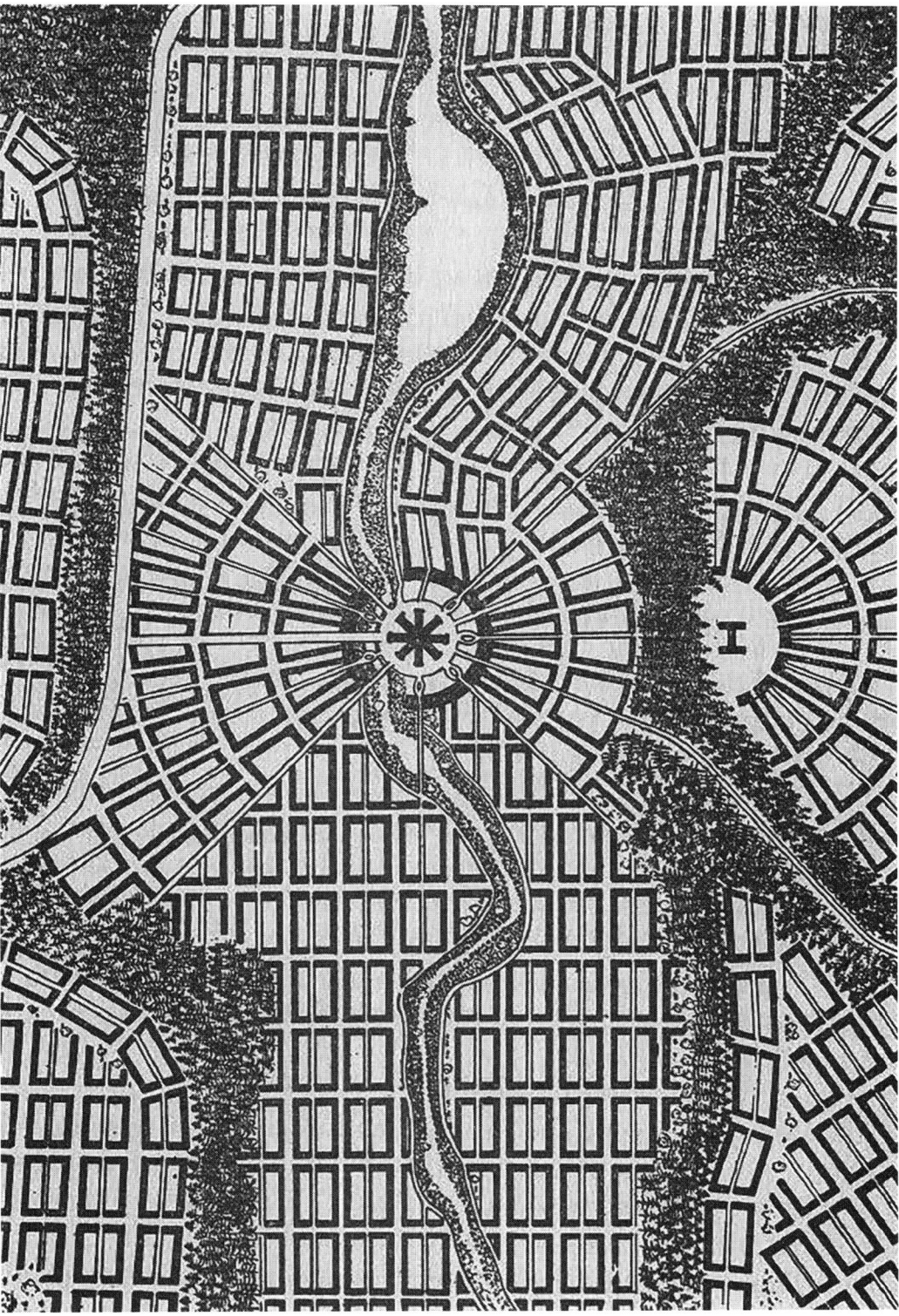

Alice Constance Austin, "Civic Center," from *The Next Step*, 1935.

CIVIC CENTER.
GRAPHIC SCALE

CIVIC CENTER
A ASSEMBLY HALL
B ADMINISTRATION
C LIBRARY & POSTOFFICE
D WOMANS SPECIALTIES
E WOMANS CLUB
F THEATRE
G MENS CLUB
H MENS SPECIALTIES
J BANK

BUILDINGS
1 RESTAURANT
2 MARKET
3 GROCERIES
4 LIGHT MANUFACTURING
5 CHURCH
6 TEMPLE
7 COLLEGE
8 HIGH SCHOOL
9 JUNIOR HIGH SCHOOL
10 GRADE SCHOOL
11 ELEMENTARY SCHOOL
12 PHILOSOPHY
13 HOME & ACCESSORIES
14 GARAGE
15 OFFICES
16 DEPT STORE

3. Paulette Bernège, *Si les femmes faisaient les maisons* (Paris: Richard Lenoir, 1928), 11.
4. Gwendolen Webster, "Revisit: Frankfurt Kitchen," *Architectural Review* 1487 (December 2021/January 2022): 42.
5. Catharine E. Beecher, *A Treatise on Domestic Economy: For the Use of Young Ladies at Home, and at School* (New York: Harper & Brothers, 1842).

years was equivalent to walking from Paris to Middle Asia.[3] The search for a balance between objects and the environment, and between individual interests and collective consequences, is gender nonspecific, but it definitely lies in the hands of those who are struggling with the results (usually women).

The Home Improvement Movement and Domestic Science promoted by these social and environmental reformers were never just about the house. Even less were they about kitchens or women. Margarete Schütte-Lihotzky, known as the mother of all fitted kitchens, in particular the mass-produced Frankfurt Kitchen, said at the end of her life, "If I'd known people would do nothing but talk about the damn kitchen, I wouldn't have invented it."[4] When the domestic reformers considered the house, they focused on the quality of air and water, the quantity of gas needed to prepare food, the amount of arsenic in wallpaper, the toxic ingredients in home goods, the trees outside, and the neighbors. In Beecher's *A Treatise on Domestic Economy*, published in 1842, the house was related to everything that came into and out of it, and

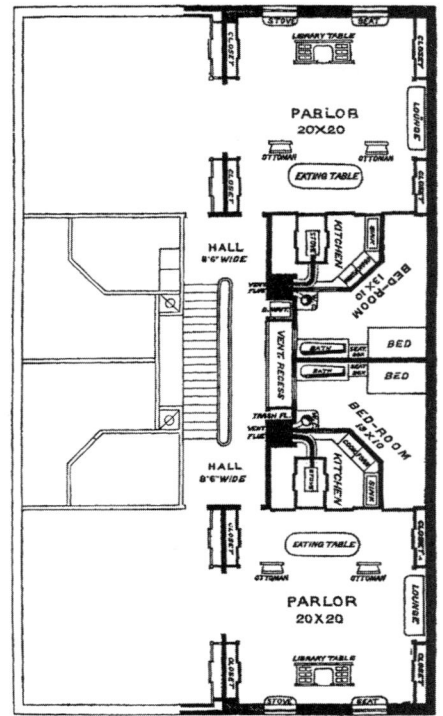

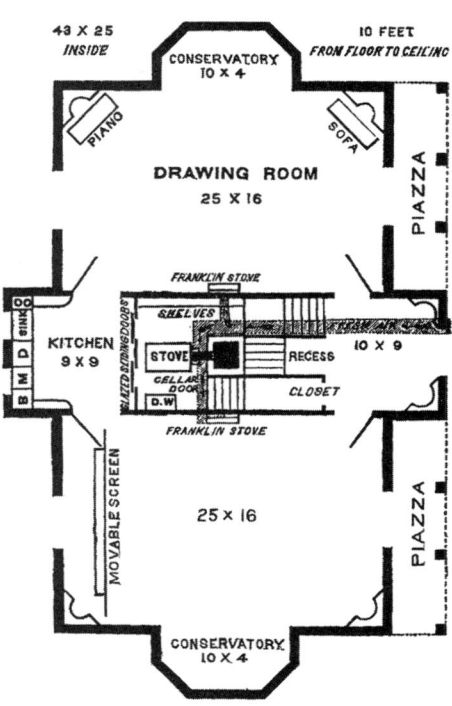

Catharine Beecher and Harriet Beecher Stowe. The plans make innovative use of sliding doors and movable screens to create adaptable spaces. From *The American Woman's Home: Or, Principles of Domestic Science*, 1869.

was part of the community considered as a whole.[5] Beecher presented drawings of bodily organs, information on staircases, soaps, furniture, clothing, and posture, establishing parallels between living entities, spaces, and activities. In her understanding of objects as being in an interlaced system, architecture was translated into contexts beyond mere buildings. Extending the bounds of architecture's jurisdiction to outside a building's four walls led to recognizing architecture as an element responsible for life expectancy as well as the depletion of resources. The undertakings of the domestic reformers provided solutions to reduce dust, dismiss corset dresses, and maintain a comfortable indoor temperature with minimum expenditure. Furthermore, this led to questioning the implications of decisions made by architects who had never cleaned or used most of what they had designed and did not care about what happened next.

The contributions of the domestic reformers include a vast array of projects, such as the first layout of an open-plan with movable partitions, published by Beecher in 1869 – which included a garbage chute, ventilation shafts, dumbwaiters, sliding doors, storage walls, as well as spaces for education and social gatherings, horticulture, and beekeeping – years before the masters of the Modern Movement designed flexible and

6. Catharine Beecher and Harriet Beecher Stowe, *The American Woman's Home: Or, Principles of Domestic Science* (New York: J. B. Ford & Co., 1869), 443, 456, 457.
7. Ellen Henrietta Richards, *Euthenics, the Science of Controllable Environment; A Plea for Better Living Conditions as a First Step Toward Higher Human Efficiency* (Boston: Whitcomb & Barrows, 1910).
8. Charlotte Perkins Gilman, "Applepieville," *Independent*, September 25, 1920, 365.

well-equipped spaces.[6] Another contribution, the Cooperative Housekeeping Association, founded by Fay Peirce in 1870, promoted shared services based on an understanding of the relationships between houses, neighborhoods, time, money, resources, and responsibilities. Other examples include: the concept of euthenics,[7] developed by Richards as the science for the improvement of living conditions, and Applepieville,[8] a rural community imagined by Perkins Gilman to prevent social isolation and promote the benefit of shared services.

These authors envisioned cities in which development is not a synonym for the destruction of anything or anyone. Feeling the urge to change the way they lived, they changed the history of architecture. They created alternatives to the ways resources and time are consumed. For example, unlike Taylorism, the system of scientific management for speeding up work, successful management was not, according to Moller Gilbreth, the way to make the best of a task but to make the best of a person. She devoted decades to introducing the "human element" into design, adjusting the height of work spaces so disabled people could do their jobs comfortably, and celebrating the creative misuse of standardized objects, such as a door hinge that a one-armed person could use to open a bottle cap. By developing body-centered, anti-fatigue designs that revealed common but invisible needs, she made care the main definition for a deep understanding of long-term efficiency.

The relations between architecture, nature, and living beings is usually limited to visual considerations or to an aesthetic based on model proportions, a standardized focal point, and a false idea of symmetry associated with nature. Contrary to this, the domestic reformers understood these relations as interdependent systems. In their writings and plans, humans appear truly alive for the first time. Considering the human body as an interdependent organ in charge of the maintenance of spaces went hand in hand with contemplating the design not of objects or pieces but of systems as a whole. For them, the body was an aging sensorial apparatus linked to its surroundings and attached in many different ways to other living entities. Demanding balance and parity over the goal for power, they spoke of *mutualism, interactions, reciprocal adaptations*, and *cooperation*, anticipating the principles of *coevolution*, a term coined in 1964 that describes a concept of natural dependencies. The domestic reformers considered architecture a common project and the core of care. Their interest in the collective nature of habitation confronted the

A - CHURCH
B - TOWN HALL
C - POST OFFICE - BANK
D - STORES
E - SCHOOL
F - PLAYGROUND - POOL
G - COMMUNITY HOUSE
H - STORES
I - LIBRARY or STORES
K - BAND STAND

Charlotte Perkins Gilman, Applepieville, 1920. Perkins Gilman used her speculative fiction, published in the magazine *The Independent*, to refine her vision of an ideal city.

idea of architecture as the creation of individual universes in which living entities, materials, food, and territory were not seen as part of the same network. The intentions of these reformers were to minimize the burdens of buildings and to understand architecture not by its physical presence.

Today, 100 years after the work of the domestic reformers, architecture still conceals many of the elements that sustain us. Water is hidden in pipes that are hidden inside walls; waste disposal is out of view and thus far from our responsibility; our relationship with the environment is often behind glass, as is our connection with others. For many, heat comes on during cold winters, packages land on doorsteps, and sewage vanishes outside. But where is outside? Where can trash be transported so it no longer is ours? Learning from the domestic reformers, we need to extend the definition of "user" to include those who carry and turn materials into spaces, those who remove garbage from buildings and those who are outside. Addressing the invisible in architecture means considering the interdependencies of different elements and entities, between resources and activities, and to bring to light what architecture has been hiding for decades: our relationship with the elements that define our subsistence. Anything less than this is incomplete.

Fernanda Canales is an architect in Mexico. She has a PhD from Escuela Técnica Superior de Arquitectura de Madrid and has taught at Yale, Princeton, Harvard, and the Politecnico di Milano.

Observations on a Good Place

Between the Queensboro and the Brooklyn bridges, the eastern shore of the East River is one of the fastest changing faces of New York. In 2017, the city's Economic Development Corporation rebranded this run-down postindustrial landscape as the "Innovation Coast." The branding, originally an attempt, in part, to lure Amazon to build its second headquarters in the city, is now apt to describe the iconic, and at times gimmicky, architecture that has sprung up to house both tech companies and their well-compensated workers: OMA's cantilevered boxes at Eagle and West streets, Gensler and HWKN's extruded cross-section cut at 25 Kent, ODA's glassy glaciers at 420 Kent and their ornately faceted Soho Works, to name a few. Among these photogenic icons, a new public project stands out for its refusal to pose for photographs and commitment to place-making basics over formal innovation.

In the midst of this rapid development, Domino Square, designed by Studio Cadena with Field Operations, opened in September in Williamsburg, Brooklyn. A one-acre plaza nestled between PAU's Domino Sugar Refinery to the north, Selldorf Architects' porcelain-clad towers to the south, and SHoP's doughnut-shaped housing to the east, it is simply a half amphitheater that looks toward the Manhattan skyline. From

Studio Cadena with Field Operations, Domino Square, Williamsburg, Brooklyn, 2024. The square completes the Domino Park waterfront redevelopment along the East River, around the former sugar refinery. Photo: Patrick Templeton.

the amphitheater seating, one can see the Statue of Liberty, four miles away, framed by the Williamsburg Bridge, which soars over the East River just on the other side of the new Selldorf apartments. In the center is a gravel arena used for a farmers market, salsa nights, and, in winter, ice-skating. It's occupied by moveable chairs and tables and shaded by a suspended canopy. Around this amphitheater, raised beds filled

with trees and shrubs soften the spartan Corten steel and concrete. Underneath is a loggia, running along the sidewalk, with small retail spaces for future vendors. Rather than creating another iconic tourist attraction – which is the Hudson Yards or High Line model – the designers provide an adaptable and habitable reprieve. Domino Square isn't much to look at, but it's a place to be. – Patrick Templeton

Manuel Álvarez Diestro

Refrigerated Air

Air conditioners are relatively simple devices. They are also in high demand. The International Energy Agency's 2018 study "The Future of Cooling" estimated there were 1.6 billion air conditioners in the world. Driven by demand in developing countries, where temperatures, and sometimes incomes, are rising, this will grow to 5.6 billion units by 2050. That's 10 air conditioners sold every second for 30 years.

To cool an interior, a unit's fan blows the room's warm, often humid air over tubes that carry a refrigerant. When the warmed refrigerant travels through the tubes to the compressor and condenser, located outside, the heat is wrung out of it. The cycle then repeats. In other words, air conditioners cool interior environments by warming the exterior one. The warming effect of this heat transfer, however, pales in comparison to the global warming caused by the greenhouse gases produced in generating the electricity air conditioners need to run. As of 2022, 1,950 million tons of CO_2, or 3.94 percent of total global greenhouse gas emissions, are released annually to produce the energy for AC.

The method of electromechanically moving heat was developed in the early 20th century in the US, where it quickly became ubiquitous. The first air conditioner was installed in a vacant house in Minneapolis in 1914; the first window unit went on sale in 1932 for the small fortune of $10,000; ultimately, AC made Las Vegas possible. And made cooler interiors possible around the world. As a result, time-tested passive cooling strategies are all but lost. Once ubiquitous awnings, which can reduce heat gain on south- and west-facing windows by up to 80 percent, are often considered ugly or unfashionable today. Night-flushing – opening windows to let the cool night air in and the warm air out – has been forgotten, or is no longer an option due to higher temperatures and humidity. Today, researchers around the world are working to develop a more energy efficient way of cooling the air that focuses on lowering humidity. As the *Washington Post* reported this fall, citing an engineer working to bring "more planet-friendly air conditioners to homes," air-conditioning is "a necessity product in the context of today's world." – *The Log Editors*

Manuel Álvarez Diestro is a Spanish photographer and filmmaker.

I took this photo in 2019 as I went up to the top of an apartment block in Bangkok, Thailand. I was intrigued by how the aircon system overlooks the city. Top: In the tourist city of Benidorm, Spain, in 2020, there was no sign of human interaction during the pandemic, just repetitive AC units.

AC units and a few awnings dominate the facade of this apartment building in
Caracas, Venezuela, 2014.

Pipes and AC units mingle in a state of decay in the interior courtyard of this
building in Yangon, Myanmar, 2018.

In Quarry Bay, Hong Kong, a residential and business district, air conditioners populate the facade, adding to the already dense feeling of the area, 2023. Top: I took this photo in 2019. I had visited the same district of Puerto Madero, Buenos Aires, two decades before there was anything built besides the old dock. Now it's an upper-class residential neighborhood.

I took this photo in Beirut, Lebanon, in 2006, right after that war between Hezbollah and Israel.

In Seoul, near the central railway station, AC units nearly cover a building's
facade, 2019.

There's something disconcerting, even dispiriting, about Rome–Las Vegas: Bread and Circuses, a new book of photographs by Iwan Baan. Maybe it's because the first time I visited Rome – in 1970 – I fell in love with all of it. Mass with the Pope at St. Peter's, chatting (in French) with nuns in the convent above the Spanish Steps, the waiter Antonio, with his blue eyes and blue Vespa, even the soldiers with machine guns at the airport. I've been back many times.

Or maybe my trip to Las Vegas in 2007. I went with a friend who was attending a shopping center convention. I laughed out loud when we entered Caesar's Palace to check in, rolled my eyes at the colors of the sky inside the Venetian, saw a Cirque du Soleil show, and tried a slot machine while sipping the obligatory cocktail. It was fun, but I've not been back.

Rome and Las Vegas are both taught in schools of architecture as emblematic of human civilization. In fact, Rome–Las Vegas is a photographic follow-up of sorts to Learning From Las Vegas (1972). But the gold-mirror ink on the cover of the saddle-stitched, overstuffed pages seems to poke fun at the whole undertaking. The Vegas photos are glossy; Rome photos are matte. Turn the pages and Baan's signature aerial photos zoom in on streets and landmarks, then in on details, including the overexposed bodies of tourists (think Eameses' Powers of Ten). Lindsay Harris, who initiated the project for a 2022 exhibition at the American Academy in Rome,

Las Vegas photos in Iwan Baan, *Rome–Las Vegas: Bread and Circuses.* With essays by Lindsay Harris, Izzy Kornblatt, and Ryan Scavnicky. Design: Haller Brun. Lars Müller, 2024. 320 pages.

writes, "Baan tells visual stories about Las Vegas and Rome." But what kinds of stories?

As if replying, Ryan Scavnicky quotes Nikola Tesla: "You may yet live to see man-made horrors beyond your comprehension." Then he adds, "In this book, the city of global tourism is presented as a horror." This may be why the "stories" in Rome–Las Vegas are disconcerting. When tourists drape themselves around the Trevi Fountain or when the Las Vegas Sphere is cast as a yellow emoji, the very story of what we now call architectural culture is called into question. – Cynthia Davidson

Lachlan Summers

A Building Is a Mouth Through Which The Earth Speaks

I haven't lived in Mexico City for about a year now, but I still feel like one of its earthquakes is about to take hold of me. When I lived there, this feeling was routine, jarred by a car horn in the distance mimicking an earthquake alert; a passing truck shaking my building; sudden ripples in my glass of water. Anything could be a sign that the Earth had returned. I attribute this partly to my research: since the city's 2017 earthquake – magnitude 7.1 – I conducted ethnographic research in Mexico City for about five years – that's five years of talking almost exclusively about earthquakes. *Dogs bark when they hear sounds underground. If they bark, an earthquake might be coming. At night, there are strange lights in the sky. They sometimes appear with earthquakes. Watch out during September. The rainy season often brings earthquakes.* The demographic most affected by hypochondria is medical students; perhaps my expectations were also a psychological response to this surfeit of geological stories.

I explained my growing fear to Marcelo, who has lived in Mexico City for all of his 50-something years, and he laughed. I began talking with Marcelo in 2018, when a friend of a friend mentioned that her uncle had become "tocado" after the 2017 earthquake. *Tocado/a* literally means "touched," and is generally used like "crazy," but the term is also used to describe someone who, after experiencing an intense earthquake, develops a debilitating fear of seismicity, which manifests physiologically, psychologically, and behaviorally. But Marcelo never really seemed crazy to me. And now, even though I live in Berlin, which is at least tectonically stable, I still find myself thinking of him whenever I get those reminders from the Earth. Light fixtures rattling. A succession of Soviet-style *plattenbauten* buildings, their concrete facades looming heavily over the street. The most recent reminder was a pallet of cement from the Mexican cement manufacturer CEMEX that sat outside my Berlin apartment for a few weeks at the beginning of 2024.

Stack of Cemex cement, Moabit, Berlin, 2024. Photo: Lachlan Summers. All images courtesy the author.

Medically, Marcelo's affliction is strange. He says that the 2017 earthquake made him sick, but contemporary biomedicine's search for a single cause, and its mind-body-environment divisions, would characterize Marcelo as being affected by a psychosomatic postearthquake trauma. Earthquakes can't make you physically ill. But Marcelo says that the shaking that began in the early afternoon of September 19, 2017, never really ended. While human time and geological time are usually described as utterly distinct, two irreconcilable scales of analysis, Mexico City's residents point to their overlap. And I mean literally *point*: you can enter this overlap by visiting someone's home and watching as they trace with their finger the cracks growing in their apartment's concrete walls, or as they gesture from a safe distance toward ceilings that sag and floors that slump – those sites where geophysical forces announce that they have taken up residence.

In 2021, when Marcelo laughs at my explanation, he shakes his head in a figure-eight motion, like a corporeal infinity symbol: *yes-I-agree-but-well-not-really-because-you-know-the-thing-is*. By way of explanation, he returns to his experience of the 2017 earthquake, something he does regularly.

"It was like something kicked the entire building from underneath. It just launched up, completely up from the surface, I swear, then landed back down, *hard*, and shook and shook from side to side. I grabbed my chair with two hands." At this point in the story, Marcelo grabs his chair with both hands. "And I was looking up at this lightbulb, which was swinging like a pendulum." He looks up at the bulb above us, shaking his head as if it were still in motion. "But everything kept moving, more and more, and I couldn't focus on anything. I just closed my eyes." After a beat, he opens his eyes again, lays his hands on the table between us, and slides them around in fast, little circles. "It was as if the whole world had animated itself, everything acted, and suddenly I realized that this building would buckle and fall to pieces, that, really, it is not a building anymore, it's not solid, but rather something impermanent." Marcelo looks around his apartment, and I follow his gaze. "Now, I see it and yes, I know it's my home, but it's also not anymore. It has become something else." He raises his palms as he says this, as if petitioning his concrete walls to hold still.

Two Dualist Histories

When earth scientists explain to me how Mexico City became seismic, they rub their hands. Their histories might stretch across millions of years, but the geological and the human coincide in their bodies and gestures. "Subduction is like this," they say, driving one hand perpendicularly under the other. "Transform is like this," moving their left hand forward and right hand back, thumbs folded against their palms, index fingers rubbing.

"The Cocos [tectonic plate] is a weird one," Alejandro, a seismology PhD student at Universidad Nacional Autónoma de México (UNAM), tells me in 2019: "It's like a dog's back leg."

"Oh, I understand," I say, lying.

"It goes down, straight down, sharply under the North American [plate]," he clarifies, the back of his right hand rubbing against his index finger, "and then, all of a sudden, it kicks back up and flattens out."

The knuckles of his right hand stop against the index finger of his left, and he lifts both hands up to eye level, then slowly hyperextends his right fingers so that they bend backward, running parallel against the palm of his left hand.

"It has friction down here, where it subducts," he says, jutting his chin toward the state of Guerrero, on his right knuckles, "and then it has some friction on the underside of the North American." He wiggles the tips of the fingers on his right hand, the Valley of Mexico. "This is one of the reasons earthquakes get to Mexico City. Even though we're not really in a subduction zone, we've got two zones of friction near us."

Alejandro's history of Mexican seismicity begins 200 million years ago, with a now-extinct tectonic plate called Farallon. One of the three oceanic plates of Panthalassa, the superocean that surrounds the Earth's most recent supercontinent, Pangaea, Farallon subducts for millions of years and suddenly ruptures under the part of Pangaea that holds what is currently known as Utah. Farallon becomes several plates: the Juan de Fuca, Explorer, and Gorda plates all continue Farallon's original journey under the North American plate, itself still moving west; the Nazca plate pushes south, under the South American plate; and the Cocos, the star of Alejandro's story, wedges itself tightly between the North American, Nazca, and Pacific plates. Dragged east by the Caribbean plate while burrowing under the North American, Cocos produces the subduction zone called the Guerrero Gap, at Alejandro's knuckles, from which most of Mexico City's major earthquakes emerge.

A marine regression between 100 and 38 million years ago permits the landmass now called Mexico to raise its head above water. As vertical fractures cut through the continental crust of the North American plate and magma seeps upward through these discontinuities, a 998-kilometer-long east-west arc now known as the Trans-Mexican Volcanic Belt assembles itself, around 8,000 volcanic structures that cut Mexico in half latitudinally, from Nayarit to Veracruz. In its central section, the river Río Balsas flows south to the Pacific Ocean, hemmed in by mountains to the north, west, and east. Somewhere between 30 and 4.5 million years ago, the volcanos begin erupting, seven overlapping phases that end recently, 700,000 years ago, sealing the valley and turning it into a basin, the once-flowing water of Río Balsas pooling into five connected lakes.

"Make a V with your hands," Alejandro tells me, body and geology still one. "Now make a cup, as if you were receiving communion."

Another history of Mexico City's earthquakes begins around 11,000 years ago, when the first human inhabitants arrive in what is now called the Valley of Mexico, the central section of the Trans-Mexican Volcanic Belt. They find these five lakes, saltwater in the north and freshwater in the south, their productive ecosystems, and sediments rich in organic matter. The Indigenous inhabitants harvest and hunt, but also undertake vast hydraulic projects, building dikes and dams to manage seasonal flooding. In the 13th century, the Xaltocanmecas develop *chinampas*, an agricultural form founded on artificial islands, which is adopted by the Mexica when Tenochtitlan, Tlacopan, and Texcoco form the Triple Alliance, in 1428, and take control of Xaltocan. Their buildings are composed of stone and adobe, and they undertake massive earthworks to ensure their constructions won't sink. Mexica cosmology holds that they are living in *Nahui Ollin*, the fifth and final sun, awaiting the earthquake that would annihilate them all.

In 1519, the Castilian conquistador Hernán Cortés encounters the Valley of Mexico, describing with wonder an immense city "built on a salt lake" that "rises and falls with its tides as does the sea," then destroys it all, including the infrastructure that manages the lakes. After conquest, the seasonal flooding confounds the colonists, who recall that the Mexica had spoken of a region called Pantitlán, where, in the dry season, Mexica had been seen placing two children's hearts – an offering to Tlaloc, petitioning the god to slow the draining of the water and extend the productive season – so they begin a fruitless search for the valley's drain. Unable to locate the outlet, and fed up with the water, the colonists embark on a still-unfinished, now half-millennium-long project of building one, draining the valley themselves – a plan to reverse geology's clock 700,000 years, before the waves of volcanic eruptions sealed the southern end of the valley.

Settled into the soft soil of drained lakes – soils that liquefy during earthquakes, soils that amplify the seismic waves that emerge from the Guerrero Gap – what is and would remain one of the largest cities in the world becomes opened to geological time.

Like the earthquakes that shake Marcelo's walls, the concrete that composes them is also understood in dual histories. In an essay for *Writing Architectural History*, historian Lucia Allais and engineer Forrest Meggers write that histories of concrete are told in one of two ways: "One, the geological image of the earth being sedimented with rock; the other, a dynamic picture of human inventions being perfected daily by technicians."

Concrete is, on its surface, simple: water; aggregate, usually gravel or sand; and binder, usually cement. Cement is a combination of a calcareous material, like limestone or chalk, silica, and alumina, like what is in clay or shale. Limestone is the Earth's most common sedimentary rock, accounting for one-fifth of all known sedimentary rocks. Cement is deeply geological, but as anthropologist Sophia Roosth demonstrates in a 2014 essay in *Grey Room*, even the most geological things are not void of something like life. Calcium carbonate is produced by the process of biomineralization, whereby living organisms, typically marine, produce shells, spines, and exoskeletons. The teeth in our mouths are biomineralized. Coral reefs are another example: corals are invertebrates composed of polyps, small anthozoa akin to sea anenomes and jellyfish. The polyps of hard corals secrete calcium carbonate, the (bio)geological backbone of reefs. For the last half-billion years, much of the Earth's limestone is produced through these "biogenic" processes. When limestone is subjected to high heat, like in a volcano, and mixed with clay, a chemical reaction produces the powder we call cement; when mixed with water and aggregate, concrete.

An important feature in the history of concrete, continue Allais and Meggers, is that "making it required little exactitude." This perhaps explains why histories of cement also vary. Some begin with speculation: Robert Courland's history in his book *Concrete Planet* begins with "shamans" dancing around Neolithic fireplaces, seeking hotter and hotter flames, trying to recreate what they had witnessed lightning do to stone. Others begin with the Roman Pantheon, built in 128 CE, whose 43-meter-diameter dome is still held in place by pozzolana, a volcanic rock sourced from Naples. Still others follow the patents. English businessman James Parker, recounts Frank Newby in his book *Early Reinforced Concrete*, uses ground chalk residue from Kent beaches in 1796 to make a hydraulic binder he called "Roman Cement"; French engineer L.J. Vicat conducts experiments that showed that pozzolana is a silicate and that it reacts with lime, and then he develops an artificial pozzolana. Throughout the 19th century, so many engineers patented their own version of concrete, each according to its unique mixing ratio and the panel dimensions their ratio would sustain, that it is difficult to identify "the inventor." However, given the frenzy of interest in the material, it's easy to agree with industrialist François Coignet, who, while proposing a concrete house for the Paris Expo of 1855, declares grandly, "The reign of stone in building construction seems to have come to an end. Cement, concrete and iron are destined to replace it."

These two histories point toward concrete's peculiar position in the pantheon of architectural materials. In 1927, Frank Lloyd Wright writes of concrete:

Is it stone? Yes and no.
Is it plaster? Yes and no.
Is it brick or tile? Yes and no.
Is it cast iron? Yes and no.
Poor concrete! Still looking for its own at the hands of Man.

So shot through with dualisms – liquid/solid, natural/artificial, geological/human – its banality invites rhapsody. In his book *My Cocaine Museum*, anthropologist Michael Taussig waxes, "You start with stone. You make a powder. And then in the process of building, you add water and end up with a new form of 'stone' in accord with the shape desired. It sounds like magic but we call it technology." Geology, too, though appearing inert, invites similar wonder: "Rocks are not nouns, but verbs," geologist Marcia Bjornerud tells us in *Timefulness*; we have to shift the timescale to see their animacy. Depending on your perspective, concrete buildings in particular and geology in general are discrete things: environment and actor, material and process, effect and cause.

Domesticating Geology

"Tell me about this room, Marcelo."

"That's my son's room. He lived there until he was 20... 22. We put these big curtains here" – he jerks the thick, gray curtain around waist-level, so a wave rises to the wood bar it hangs from – "because he slept so badly as a child. He was such a light sleeper. He still is. I think he has curtains like these in his apartment now. But when he was a child, the light, the noise, he would wake up to everything."

Marcelo's apartment is in Doctores, a working-class district in central Mexico City, bordered by the busy avenues Chapultepec to the north and Cuauhtémoc to the west. The building was constructed in the 1950s, and he's lived there since the early '80s, on the fourth of five floors. Its interior is baby blue. Marcelo's son's room and a spacious living room face the street, the latter's window ledges filled with plants; in the center are a kitchen and a bathroom; a short hallway past the entry leads to two large bedrooms that abut a central atrium. Light floods in from several angles, and the street below is a vocal presence. Photos of the family at various ages hang on the walls, and in the hallway, about knee-high, are faded squiggles, where you might imagine a child, Marcelo's son, scribbling in secret. When I first visit Marcelo, his home seems idyllic.

In his 1516 book *Utopia*, Thomas More imagines a whole city built of concrete. A work of satire, the first volume describes the social life of 16th-century England, the second details a dialogue between More and Raphael Hythloday, a fictious traveler who describes the social, political, and economic conditions of an island called Utopia – a neologism that uses Ancient Greek to say "no place" but now means "good place." The island had, Hythloday tells More, recently undergone an architectural upgrade:

The first houses were low . . . built slapdash out of any sort of lumber . . . but now their houses are all three storeys high and handsomely constructed; the outer sections of the walls are made of fieldstone, quarried rock or brick, and the space between is filled up with gravel and cement. The roofs are flat and are covered with a kind of cement which is cheap but so well mixed that it is impervious to fire and superior to lead in defying the damage caused by storms.

Concrete's association with an ideal society helps the material boom at the turn of the 20th century. New dualisms proliferate: ancient and modern; malleable but fixed; rapid, yet permanent. The Hoover Dam, on the Colorado River, offers one such example. Built in five years, the dam is composed of 3.4 million cubic meters of concrete, a feat of engineering that dwarfs human senses. In her essay "At the Dam," Joan Didion wonders "what it was about the dam that made me think of it at times and in places where I once thought of the Mindanao Trench, or of the stars wheeling in their courses, or of the words *As it was in the beginning, is now and ever shall be, world without end, amen.*" The awe is intentional: Oskar J.W. Hansen, who wins a competition to sculpt the dam's monuments, also designs a celestial map, which adorns the floor of its viewing plaza. Using the "universal language of the stars," Hansen explains, to deny "the oblivion imposed by time," the map depicts the position of the stars so that future visitors to Earth, who might have different time-keeping practices, would read their position and know when the dam had been inaugurated: 9:30 pm, September 30, 1935. The dam is actually inaugurated at 11:00 am that day, but because stars are not visible in the daytime, Hansen pushes the hands of his eternal clock forward a few hours.

Concrete materializes in perpetuity in postrevolutionary Mexico, when, as historian Mauricio Tenorio-Trillo puts it in *I Speak of the City*, "modernity, nationalism, and secular prog-ress were a question of facades." While concrete and cement were used in Mexico during the Porfiriato, the dictatorship of Porfirio Díaz from 1876 to 1911, concrete's permanence offers a means of materializing the ideologies and objec-tives of the new revolutionary government. After a decade of civil war (1910–1920), concrete proves both a practical mode of rebuilding the country and, in the footsteps of European modernist architects like Le Corbusier and Walter Gropius, an architectural break with the Porfiriato. In 1909, three years after Cementos Hidalgo opens, Mexican cement produc-tion amounts to 66,000 tons per year. But with government investment, concrete proliferates: in 1931, when Cementos Hidalgo and Cementos Portland Monterrey join to form Cementos Mexicanos, CEMEX, the Mexican state is spending around 73 percent of its coffers on roads, highways, schools, and hospitals, much of it built with concrete. Population growth, writes geographer Matthew Fry, goes "hand-in-hand with the spread of concrete blocks." In 1940, when Mexico City's metropolitan population is around two million, CEMEX produces 484,992 tons of cement; by 1970, when the population is around 9.1 million, production averages 7.2 million tons per year. As Mexico's economy centralizes in the capital, Mexico City is converted, in poet Octavio Paz's words, into "a monstrous, inflated head, crushing the frail body that sustains it." This is not only figurative. With the weight of the concrete and the overuse of the underground aquifer, Mexico City begins plummeting into the lakebed's soft soil at a rate of about 60 centimeters per year.

El cemento
en la Revolución Constructiva
de México

"Cement in the constructive revolution of México," *El Nacional*, November 20, 1933.

Literature scholar Rubén Gallo suggests that while other new technologies, such as cameras and radios, would invite reflection on future utopias, "cement was initially ignored by the Mexican intelligentsia." Concerned by a disinterest in their material, Mexican cement makers form, in 1923, the Comité para Propagar el Uso del Cemento Portland (Committee to Promote the Use of Portland Cement) in order to foster, in Gallo's words, "the cultural use of cement." Among other forms of proselytizing, the committee publishes the magazine *Cemento*. Similar magazines circulate in Europe, with *Le Ciment* (1896) and *Le Béton Armé* (1898) in France, and *Beton und Eisen* (1902) in Germany. Roland Hall, a publicist from the US who had managed earlier advertising campaigns with the Alpha Portland Cement Company, assists the young Mexican-US publicist Federico Sánchez Fogarty to hype up concrete. Under Sánchez's editorship, *Cemento* is distributed monthly from 1925 to 1930, beginning with 8,000 copies and quickly reaching 12,000, aimed at an audience of, according to the committee, "government officials, priests, industrialists, agriculturalists, business people, general professionals, construction workers, property owners and future property owners." Writing as himself and under various pen names, Sánchez aims to aestheticize concrete and to convince Mexico that cement is not *tierra molida* (ground dirt) but rather *polvo mágico* (magic dust).

Paralleling the revolutionary government's ideology of *mestizaje*, the racial admixture that produced the *raza cósmica* (cosmic race), concrete is also a mixture for Mexico's future. "Is concrete not a conglomeration of stone and iron and cement? And is not cement in turn a conglomerate of lime and mud?" asks Sánchez. "What is it if not the past united with the present in the manufacture of the future?" Geology is no longer a context but a *tool*. With its correct use, concrete wouldn't only spotlight the endurance of structures past but also their permanence into the future. Sánchez writes: "Mixed with adequate materials in appropriate proportions, it resists all forces of destruction. It is more solid than many of the rocks that agglomerate in the mountains."

Meditating upon concrete's permanence, Sánchez often weighs in on time. "Can cement call itself eternal?" he asks, on cement's behalf, in *Cemento* 8/9. "We do not think the expression appropriate, because that word is applicable to what has no absolute beginning or end; it belongs, therefore, to religion." And yet, he continues, "the adjectives 'permanent' and 'stable' are too moderate in the evaluation of a

LA FUENTE DEL TIEMPO

El tiempo es un destructor implacable - todo lo apolilla, carcome o enmohece - todo menos el concreto.

El concreto, entre más años pasan, es mejor.

Exija usted que cimientos, paredes y techos sean de concreto, y de estuco las fachadas.

"Time is a relentless destroyer – it gnaws on, eats away at, and renders moldy everything – everything except concrete," in "The Source of Time," *Cemento* 8/9 (August and September 1925).

concrete building." Concrete would withstand everything, he suggests, even time itself.

Today, most buildings in Mexico City are built using "permanent" materials, which is to say, concrete. CEMEX presently has the capacity to produce 92 million tons of cement per year, making it the third-largest cement manufacturer in the world – between 1988 and 2015, this company alone produced 0.04 percent of the world's carbon emissions. Fifty percent of CEMEX's cement is used for housing; since 2000, 81 percent of Mexico's new housing is built with concrete. Government regulations incentivize the material's use: qualification for state-funded, low-income housing mortgages require that the house be built with a "permanent" material, seeing concrete usurp traditional materials like adobe. Though adobe better endures the region's seismicity than concrete, it requires upkeep, so it's classified as "temporary."

Tlatelolco, in central Mexico City, is a place known by three names. First, La Plaza de las Tres Culturas (The Three Cultures Plaza), so named for a square designed by Mario Pani and built in 1966 that draws attention to the site's mixture of preconquest, Spanish colonial, and independent Mexican architecture. The second is "Tlatelolco," taking the name of that preconquest city-state, which becomes the dominant title after October 2, 1968, when the military opens fire on a student protest, killing some 400 people 10 days before Mexico City would open the Olympic Games. The final name, though seldom used, is El Conjunto Urbano Presidente Aldolfo López Mateos (The Urban Housing Complex of President Adolfo López Mateos), which names a middle-class housing complex built under the presidency of López Mateos (1958–1964). Also designed by Mario Pani, the complex draws upon Le Corbusier's functionalist conception of urban life, whereby the rational use of city space improves urban hygiene. In a 1950 essay, Pani writes, "This is how one builds a nation: by purifying the putrefaction and constructing new homes on the clean and redeemed terrain." Throughout his career, Pani designs and directs 130 such complexes, working also on schools and hospitals.

Like Pani's other projects, El Conjunto Urbano is designed and built almost entirely with reinforced concrete. The association of reinforced concrete with earthquake safety might be traced to the English cement manufacturer Ernest Ransome, who moves to San Francisco in the late 19th century, opens an architectural firm around the corner from the

Nuevo León, an apartment building in El Conjunto Urbano Presidente Aldolfo López Mateos, in Tlaltelolco, Mexico City, destroyed by the earthquake of September 19, 1985. Photo: Marco Antonio Cruz/Imagen Latina.

California Portland Cement Company, and patents twisted iron bar reinforcements in concrete panels and columns. San Francisco's 1906 earthquake demonstrates their durability – reinforced concrete buildings survive both the tremors and the fires that follow. After the 1923 Kanto earthquake, in which 140,000 people are killed across Tokyo and Yokohama, only reinforced concrete structures remain, confirming to engineers that seismic zones demand reinforced concrete. The strength of the material lies in its ductility: by distributing lateral forces and loads across the components of the structure, the building can move with an earthquake, rather than brace rigidly against it. During an earthquake, a building secures itself by becoming more continuous with the Earth.

El Conjunto Urbano comprises 102 buildings, with 12,000 apartments and some 90,000 residents. One of these buildings collapses at 7:19 am, September 19, 1985, when an earthquake strike in the Guerrero Gap, travels across the crust of southern Mexico to Mexico City, then shakes its soft soil for 90 seconds. In the building that falls, 628 people are crushed to death. Another 27 buildings in the complex are damaged and eventually demolished. Across the city, 300 buildings collapse immediately, 500 more are soon demolished; 40,000 people are killed, and another 250,000 are left without housing. The ruins of fallen buildings reveal widespread use of shoddy materials and unsound construction

45

practices, most conspicuously in government buildings, such as public housing and hospitals. In a 2011 article for *Nature* titled "Corruption Kills," engineers Nicholas Ambraseys and Roger Bilham describe the ease with which corruption shapes buildings: "The assembly of a building, from the pouring of foundations to the final coat of paint, is a process of concealment, a circumstance ideally suited to the omission or dilution of expensive but essential structural components." At magnitude 8.1, the 1985 earthquake is the most destructive natural event in the region's recorded history.

The seismic waves that hit Mexico City in 1985 have a two-second period. All earthquakes have their own temporal signature, their period, which is to say the duration of the cycles between the peaks and troughs of their seismic waves. Buildings, too, have their own time, called their natural frequency, which is largely determined by their height. One way to visualize this is to imagine a boat. A small boat can be shaken by small waves, but will ride up over large waves; a cargo ship, conversely, can plough through choppy waves, but will be tipped over by large ones. When the size of the ocean wave and the size of the ship coincide, it topples. Likewise, there's a relationship between the natural time of a building and the time of the earthquake: should the two coincide, the building will enter a state called resonance, in which the building itself amplifies the waves that have come from the Earth. Determining a building's natural frequency in a place like Mexico City is difficult, because the soft soils elongate a building's natural frequency. But in 1985, the time of the earthquake and the time of the building coincide in structures between six and 15 stories, a typical height for residences, which enter their resonance frequency, and collapse.

Reinforced concrete is permanent, unless it is in contact with the atmosphere. As Ransome tours San Francisco, pointing out to residents the reinforced concrete structures that still stand after the 1906 earthquake, researchers from the University of Tokyo also visit, taking samples from the reinforced concrete structures that had fallen. They discover something horrifying. That reinforced concrete had some architectural deficiencies is known – rebar rusts, expands, and cracks the concrete – but the physical mechanism by which rust forms is not. Rainwater is often blamed – it must be seeping into the concrete, these accounts say, oxidizing the bar – so a solution would call for less porous concrete, concrete that better isolates the bar from the outside world. But in 1928, Minoru Hamada and Yoshikazu Uchida publish

The uncertain, potentially widening gap between neighboring buildings seen from José Enrique's Colonia Guerrero apartment, Mexico City, 2022. Photo: Lachlan Summers.

an article, in Japanese, that argues that while limestone's high pH should, indeed, prevent oxidation, concrete actually *absorbs* CO_2, lowering its pH. Concrete itself rusts the bars that reinforce it, which, in turn, expand and crack the concrete. The collapse of reinforced concrete is not a question of if, but when: the time it takes is determined by the concrete's porosity and its thickness. Forty years later, Hamada publishes these findings again, in English, and they rapidly circulate, providing the foundation for the discipline of materials science, and sharing with engineers of the world the equation $T = KX2$: reinforced concrete, the eternal stone, has a useful life of about 100 years.

Concrete seems enduring, but that might only be because it conceals what a building is really up to. And while concrete is resilient against pressure, it has low tensile strength. This is to say, it can withstand the pressure of "a bull elephant standing on a coin," as energy historian Vaclav Smil puts it, in an essay for *Spectrum*, but is "weaker than human skin" at resisting pulling forces. When concrete cracks, its useful life ends. Instead of distributing an earthquake's shaking, cracked concrete moves out of sync with the rest of the building, concentrating the earthquake's forces in specific regions. In an essay titled "Viscosity in Matter, Life and Sociality," anthropologist Cristián Simonetti writes that "the fixity that, to modern eyes, concrete appears to grant, is in truth but transitory. Not only does concrete deform under pressure; it is also bound to melt back into the cycle of rock formation whence it originated."

Geologizing Domesticity

José Enrique has begun most days since the 2017 earthquake the same way: "I wake up to my alarm, come here, open the curtains, and check to see if the gap has widened. Then I go to work." He motions with his head to the neighboring building, and I look through his window. There is definitely a gap, but I can't tell if it is really widening toward the top or if it's just an illusion of perspective. I stare at the gap for a little while, then take a photo, and stare at that. José Enrique inflates his cheeks and exhales, whistling slightly, then assures me that it is widening, that he sees it every day and keeps track of it. In his early 60s, from central Mexico City, José Enrique refers to himself as having become tocado after the earthquake, that he feels like he can now more easily notice buildings that have become perilous. A few weeks after the earthquake, he sees that the building across the atrium had lost touch with the wall adjacent to it, perhaps having

A protest by the group Damnificados Unidos de Tlalpan, marking the one-year anniversary of the 2017 earthquake, in front of a building that was destroyed by it, Tlalpan, Mexico City, 2018. Photo: Lachlan Summers.

released its grip on the foundations below; now, he lives in a state of ambient fear. As we leave the window, he glances at me, then closes the curtains.

Political scientists sometimes ask the "10 truck question" to ascertain a population's perception of state corruption during humanitarian disasters. It's a simple method. Imagine that, after a disaster, 10 trucks were to arrive, fully stocked with food, aid, medicine, and technology from international donors. How many would you expect to be stolen by public officials? And how many would you tolerate being stolen?

After the 1985 earthquake, new architectural codes and disaster prevention legislation are promulgated in Mexico City, retrofitting buildings with braces, and mandating new norms regarding height, proximity to neighboring buildings, and the minimum sizes of support beams and columns. In 1997, the city gains the right to elect its own *Jefe de Gobierno* (essentially mayor), which until then had been appointed by presidential decree, and the city elects a left-wing candidate who had risen to prominence with the postearthquake political uprisings. That same year, after these architectural reforms and improvements to disaster preparation and democratic representation, researchers ask Mexico City's residents how many of the 10 trucks would be stolen, and how many would they tolerate. They expect three would be stolen, but would tolerate zero.

In many ways, Mexico City is better prepared in 2017 than it had been for prior earthquakes. Fewer buildings collapse and the state's emergency response is better organized. Moreover, the earthquake itself is different. It emerges

internally to the North American plate, a result of pressure
placed on it by a subduction earthquake two weeks earlier.
Closer and shallower than the earthquakes that typically affect
the city, the 2017 earthquake is a much higher frequency, so
its period coincides with that of buildings much smaller than
those affected by distant, long-period subduction earthquakes.
Buildings that had historically proven themselves able to han-
dle the region's earthquakes suddenly enter their resonance
frequency and collapse.

But the 2017 earthquake reveals that the problems of 1985
had not been left in the past. The civil society group Mexicanos
Contra la Corrupción y la Impunidad (Mexicans Against
Corruption and Impunity) undertakes a systematic investigation of fallen buildings, and finds corruption and negligence
at the root of most. Clandestine helicopter pads; heavy bill-
boards on buildings long after the government had sched-
uled their removal; a primary school whose director had built
a secret fourth story that fell on her students – the ruins of
fallen buildings once again demonstrate that their sudden collapse had been long prefigured. And long anticipated: in the
five years leading up to the earthquake, residents lodge at least
6,000 construction violation complaints with the Mexico City
government. Though 32 years had passed, the political causes
of 1985 remain abidingly present.

One year after the 2017 earthquake, the researchers who
had surveyed Mexico City's residents in 1997 return, asking
again how many of the 10 trucks would be stolen, and how
many residents would tolerate. They now expect that officials
would steal six trucks, of which they would tolerate three.

A plastic sheet closes off a room occupied by the "Earth," Colonia Navarte, Mexico City, 2023. Photo: Lachlan Summers.

Since 2017, many buildings might be falling throughout Mexico City, typically in the central and eastern regions. Consider the building in Roma Norte, a middle-class district that sits between Marcelo's and José Enrique's apartments. Here, seismicity, subsidence, weathering, decay, and corruption have converged to produce a building whose foundations have given way, a building sinking unevenly into the soft soil and looming heavily over everything nearby. Such structures are dangerous to occupants, neighbors, and pedestrians. I hear stories of buildings that have given way years or even decades after being damaged in an earthquake. Because residents know that the city's architectural codes are routinely subverted, they expect that the concrete in Mexico City's buildings will come to a premature end of its useful life.

For José Enrique, the neighboring building registers on his body, as if exerting pressure on him, but it also demands that he reorganize the domestic life of his apartment around the architectural death of his own building. Prior to the earthquake, the room adjacent the now-falling building was José Enrique's bedroom; after the earthquake, he saw the gap, and moved into the spare bedroom, out of fear that the building adjacent would give way while he slept. His now-abandoned bedroom contains just a couple of dusty boxes and a table lying on its side, legs stretching toward the hallway.

Marcelo also tells me that since he felt his building shake, he can no longer trust it. It had survived the 1985 earthquake, but shook violently in 2017, and is now riven with cracks and dust, all of which point toward its furtive collapse. When we first meet, I notice that Marcelo lingers in doorways; when I see that he has moved a couch under a doorframe, I realize that these must be load-bearing walls that would offer protection from falling ceilings. I see similar things elsewhere, like whole rooms abandoned inside an otherwise normal apartment. Sometimes it's just a closed door, an attempt to contain the Earth with a lock, sometimes the doorway will be blocked by sheets of plastic to prevent visitors from entering. If you didn't know, it would look like a construction site, when in fact it is the opposite.

José Enrique's new bedroom is windowless and cramped, more of a large storage closet, but it's one of the only places in his apartment that sits outside the shadow of the building next door. "At least it will not land on me over here," he says, pointing one hand toward the top of the building adjacent and the other to his bed, calculating bodily the angle of collapse. "It will probably bring part of the building down, but I still might have a chance." Residents typically can't sell such homes, and few have the money to move to a new apartment, so they are trapped, suspended in the hazy overlap of the end of concrete's useful life, when it provides a home to humans, and the beginning of its useless life, as it collapses back into the Earth.

The scale of earthquakes is so immense that it can't really be comprehended. "You already know," Marcelo tells me. "You just have to wait, your feet, your eyes, they cannot do anything." During my research, I feel four earthquakes over magnitude 7, and when they happen, I try to tether my senses to something: swinging lights, rustling branches, a building in the distance, flapping cartoonishly. It is too much to be grasped directly. The same holds after an earthquake, when architecture and infrastructure point to the ongoing effects of an active Earth. Rainwater pools on paved surfaces where underground fissures induce subsidence; cracks spiral across fractured concrete walls; and buildings sink due to undermined concrete foundations. Mexico City's lively underbelly is hidden, so concrete buildings act as antennae, registering signals of unnoticed earthly motion. While it might be a trivial bump on the Earth's surface, it's hard to imagine the two were ever discrete things.

Under these conditions, even a building without conspicuous damage can lose the sense of permanence that concrete might once have offered. It becomes fragile, less assured, somehow transitory. José Enrique says to me in 2022, "I can no longer be at ease here… It is not really my home anymore," and Marcelo says, that same year, "I felt this building move in 2017, it should have fallen apart, but it did not. But it is as if I can feel it disintegrating now, it makes sounds at night when everything is quiet, I can hear it… It is already going." If concrete has a useful life of about 100 years, in Mexico City, seismicity, subsidence, weathering, and corruption conspire to foreshorten concrete's useful life and expedite what comes after. When concrete begins its useless life, the geological eternity it once promised begins seeping out into human presents.

On Geological Simultaneity

Whoever invented the ship invented the shipwreck, to paraphrase the cultural theorist Paul Virilio. For some residents of Mexico City, the echoes of an earthquake take root in their walls, ceilings, and floors, and everyday life becomes ensnared in the building's future collapse. Marcelo's and José Enrique's buildings don't only carry traces of their past damage but they also point toward the inevitability of their destruction. The writer W.G. Sebald approaches something similar in *The Rings of Saturn*, describing the buildings of Dunwich, in Britain, which fell one-by-one into the sea, eventually leading to the abandonment of the village. But rather than just natural vulnerability, the weight of the fortifications that residents built to protect themselves from the encroaching waves so overburdened the cliffs on which the town sat that they buckled, the cliffs succumbing long before they would have done from erosion alone. In *Austerlitz*, Sebald echoes this point, suggesting that buildings "cast the shadow of their own destruction before them, and are designed from the first with an eye to their later existence as ruins." Scholar Eric Santner describes this as the "essential paradox of natural history": not only do we construct buildings that inevitably fail but these constructions *solicit* those forces of failure. With destruction lying latent in the structure itself, a building is both witness to past damage and an avatar of its eventual collapse: as much what still remains as it is that which has yet to cease.

"I don't know when, but it will happen," José Enrique tells me. "It is happening." To live in architectural death, in the overlap of concrete's useful and useless lives, is to live in these two discrete but simultaneous times. The dualisms, long characteristic of concrete, return. No longer just natural and artificial, or rapid yet permanent, buildings become both human architecture and extensions of the Earth; homes and indifferent geological entities; domestic intimacy flecked with geological eternity. Living with collapse is to vacillate between these two phases, between everyday life and reminders of the Earth. If an ecotone describes spatially the overlap between two distinct ecological communities, such as the littoral zone, where waves lap at a shore, we might be able to think that temporally, a chronotone, when the geological demands to be noticed by palpably heaving and receding, saturating the human present as it does so, causing it to swell and distend.

The story goes that when André Breton, author of the *Surrealist Manifesto*, visits UNAM, in 1938, to speak about surrealism, his lecture says nothing more than, "I don't know why I came, I have nothing to teach you. Mexico is the most surreal country in the world." A walk in downtown Mexico City is a tour through surrealness, and illustrates what writer Carlos Fuentes means when he writes, in *A New Time for Mexico*, "In Mexico, there is not and never has been one single time. . . . In Mexico, all times are living, all pasts are present."

You'll make out the walls and platforms of Tenochtitlan; you'll encounter the colonial buildings, churches, and plazas that the colonists slapped on top; you'll see the centuries of construction since then, and if you look closely, you'll observe how ongoing subsidence and earthquakes fracture those structures to reveal buried architecture once lost to the Earth; in the summer, you'll follow rainwater along the banks of destroyed waterways; during earthquakes, you'll notice that the buildings on the shores of the now nonexistent lakes shake hardest; and all of this happens in the shadow of the volcanoes that have always stood vigil over the Valley of Mexico. In Mexico City, stubborn pasts and determined futures inundate the present, eroding its perimeters, loosening its grip on the immediate and perceptible.

In the buildings of Mexico City, all time is living and all pasts are present. Within the first minute of the 2017 earthquake, 44 buildings collapse; in one of the final counts, 24,581 are damaged and some 3,300 declared uninhabitable – which isn't to say that they are now uninhabited. I have seen data for 33 of those first 44 buildings, and, ranging in age from a few months to 74 years, they collectively spent 1,205 years upright in the city. But where we might be inclined to understand a building as a process, as literally build-*ing* – by resisting weathering, holding itself up, working against the forces that would return it to the Earth – in Mexico City, subsidence, graft, weathering, and seismicity convert buildings into builts: not exactly past tense, but prematurely conscripted into their future return to Earth. If, in the 1920s, Sánchez says that concrete unites the past with the present in order to produce eternity, now concrete's past transforms Mexico City's present into the terminus of an onrushing geological future.

When I think of how Marcelo and José Enrique live in buildings that are both home and "something else," I understand them as grappling with a present that has dilated beyond comprehension. The present, in the Spanish as in the English, is typically understood as the moment directly available to perception. It is pure immediacy; there is no degree. In Spanish, the past and the future are entitled to greater or lesser amounts: you can say *hace mucho tiempo* (literally: it does lots of time) or *hace poco tiempo* (it does little time) to talk about an event's distance in the past; you can say, conversely, *No lo voy a hacer por mucho tiempo* (I won't do it for lots of time). In the English, the past and future are given spatial gradations: it happened a *short* while ago; it will not happen for a *long* time. But in neither language can you say that there is more or less present: the present cannot have dimension. You can be more *in* the present, but you can't have more *of* that present; as a temporal unit, the present is a plenum.

People who are tocado/a are often told that they are crazy because they are fixated on the possibility of future earthquakes. But when you listen, they say that, in fact, the past earthquake hasn't really ended. Through concrete, the present dilates, so an earthquake can't really end. That a building is falling tends to become known only after it has fallen, but for people who live with falling, who *co*-lapse with concrete, their present falters between current stability and imminent failure, everyday life and abyssal geology, human domesticity and earthly eternity. To live in a building that is a home and a geological thing is to be stretched out between two dimensions of the present. A proximate present – immediate, perceptible, and ephemeral – flanked by a remote present – distant, extensive, and protracted. As the geophysical echoes of an earthquake take up residence in peoples' homes, human presents and geological presents coincide, the two discrete but simultaneous.

In the west of Berlin, there's a place now called Teufelsberg, literally Devil's Mountain, the city's tallest hill. One of its beginnings is in November 1937, when, in a cleared part of Grunewald Forest, Adolf Hitler and the architect Albert Speer lay the foundation stone for the proposed Wehrtechnische Fakultät, a military-technical college, for the Berlin Institute of Technology. Speer conceives architectural plans for all of Berlin, the proposed world capital of Germania, that would see the city not only last the 1,000 years of the Third Reich, but also that its buildings would decay and ruin with such elegance that they eventually rival the monuments of Ancient Greece and Rome. Instead, the military faculty now lies under a *Trümmerberg* (rubble mountain), one of dozens that litter Germany. In the Allied bombing campaign (1942–45), some 400,000 buildings are destroyed in Berlin, producing at least 25 million cubic meters of rubble, which is taken by train to Grunewald and used to assemble an artificial mountain, Teufelsberg. The military faculty building, however, proves too resilient to be blown up, so its frame lies there intact, under the mountain, under the weight of the former city. I sometimes see it on clear days, a swollen head lurching 80 meters above the plateau that surrounds Berlin.

Geological histories and the stories of geological things are not the background to human life. They are characters in it: the stories we tell of geology are part of the hold that geological materials have on our world. If a building is built as if it were permanent, its eventual collapse is much more destructive than something expected to be temporary. Living with the useless life of concrete is one way that planetary processes become knowable, like changing weather patterns, like fewer fish in a patch of ocean where someone has always fished, like flowers blooming earlier as seasons unmoor from the calendar. Part of the horror of concrete is not only that the material is constructed to the geological scale but also that it subjects people to destruction at the geological scale. The lives built around concrete's permanence also fall with the building.

When I see Teufelsberg in the distance, or when I catch myself in Berlin worrying about Mexican earthquakes, I think of the distributed now that Marcelo and José Enrique describe. There are signs everywhere, even from here, that our geological present is not going shortly into the past. Reinforced concrete, put into widespread use about 100 years ago, has a useful life of about 100 years. About 40 tons of concrete exist for every living person in the world, and a new ton is added per person per year. At this rate, it is projected that concrete will outweigh the biomass of all living things by 2040. What will become of all of our human geology? Like Teufelsberg, the rubble of Mexico City's 1985 earthquake is used to seal over a landfill, upon which now sits the wealthy suburb of Santa Fe; after Mexico City's 2017 earthquake, the rubble of fallen buildings is taken out to the vestigial lakes on the city's outskirts, which were always threatening to return, and buried there, sealing the ground all over again, in preparation for an airport that would ultimately never be built.

Lachlan Summers is a postdoctoral research fellow at the Max Planck Institute for the History of Science, with a PhD in cultural anthropology from the University of California Santa Cruz. He grew up in Australia and now lives in Berlin.

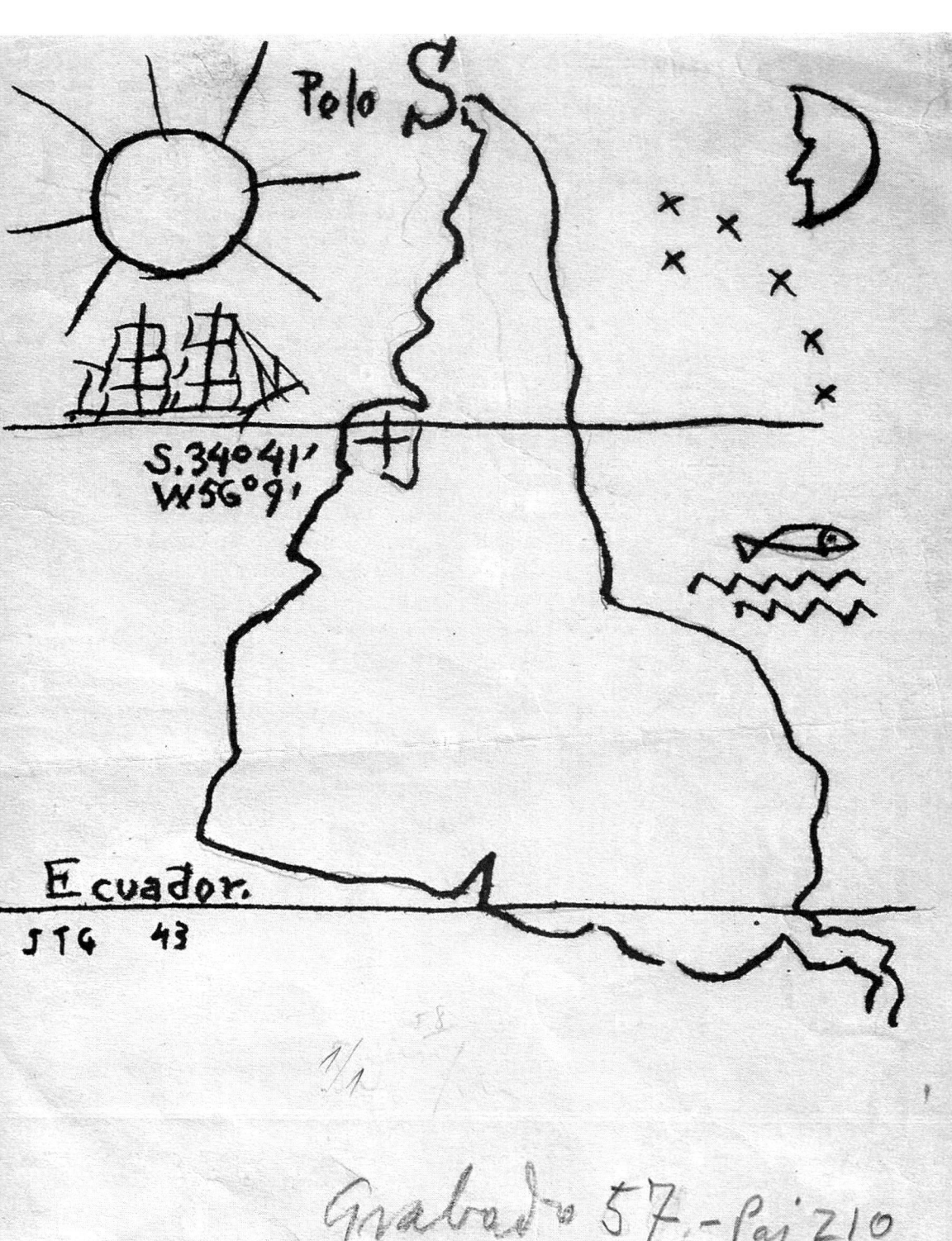

Jaime Solares Carmona

Far South

In 1943, in his sketch rotating South America 180 degrees, the Uruguayan artist Joaquín Torres-García proposed a geopolitical revolution that illustrated the radicality of the modern project in South America, encapsulated in his statement, "Our North is the South." Eight decades later, the time has come to reevaluate the significance of this reorientation and to question the extent to which the South wishes to remain a mirror image of the North – even as its antithesis. Today, it seems more interesting to move beyond the North-South dichotomy and to recognize the South within the North, and vice versa. Furthermore, it may be time to radicalize the South, intensifying what it means to be "from the South." Here, the South should be understood less as a geographical, political, or economic position and more as an epistemological frontier, a perspective grounded not in relation to but from which. Just as Latin America is the "Far West"[1] – a region that is part of Western civilization yet distant from it – South America is the extreme within the extreme: the "Far South." Being South within the South means turning in on oneself and seeking an orientation that is not given from the outside in but from reconfigurations of what it is to be here and everywhere at the same time.

This radical positionality is informed by a deep commitment to reality and a type of pragmatism that has marked contemporary South American architectural culture. Pragmatism, here, refers to an approach calibrated by the object of analysis and its practical possibilities. It is architecture's potential as informed by its making and phenomenal appearance rather than by a closed and autonomous theoretical system. This pragmatism is not driven by predefined outcomes but by a hesitant optimism that still sees the prospective dimension of architecture but without a more ambitious utopian agenda. A new generation of architectural critics embodies this spirit, formed out of a reality that has violently imposed itself over the last decade, demanding urgent political and cultural reconfigurations within the discipline.

This generation came of age in the late 2000s during the so-called Pink Tide, when local progressive governments both

1. See Alain Rouquié, *Amérique latine: Introduction à l'Extrême-Occident* (Paris: Seuil, 1987).

Opposite page: Joaquín Torres-García, *América Invertida (Inverted America)*, 1943. Ink on paper, 22 by 16 centimeters. Courtesy Fundación Torres García, Montevideo.

achieved economic growth and reduced social inequality. South America became a massive construction site fueled by the Chinese appetite for commodities such as food, minerals, and fuels. Yet this optimism would soon wane, first in the face of the global economic crises of 2008 and 2013, in the political uprisings of the early 2010s, such as those in Chile and Brazil, and then in the political backlashes culminating in events like the Bolivian military coup in 2020, not to mention the climate emergency that has intensified social inequalities and the pandemic that devoured millions of lives.

The 2016 Venice Architecture Biennale, curated by Alejandro Aravena, of Santiago, Chile, marked, in many ways, the last glimmer of hope in the political power of architecture. The architectural optimism of the 2010s has been replaced by a "trenched" optimism – a defensive stance that seeks to salvage whatever remains. Simultaneously, this period has witnessed the shedding of a certain innocence in architectural thought, which previously attempted to evade its inherent negativity. The new generation signals the end of an alignment between historiography, practice, and criticism that began in the 1990s and continued until the mid-2010s, notably around the expansion of modernist canonical studies.

This emerging generation seeks a position that is equidistant from the modernist ethos of previous generations while also distancing itself from a more radical critical approach that leans toward an "anthropologization" of architecture, often at the expense of its formal analysis. Unlike in the North, however, the theory that informs criticism has never achieved a high level of autonomy here, as it is consistently drawn back into the pressing issues of social reality. But perhaps it is precisely in this pragmatism that this criticism finds its strength, thus enhancing its ability to decipher an increasingly complex world. This criticism moves toward reality to double its realism through a pragmatic method of analysis.

Reality has become the focal point of this architectural thought. Contrary to the magical realism that characterized South American literature in the 1960s, this pragmatic realism has somewhat relinquished architecture's capacity to evoke magic. But this realism is neither naturalistic nor a mere mimetic or populist response to reality's demands. Instead, it is a "dirty realism," as defined by Liane Lefaivre in the late 1980s.[2] Dirty realism distorts and accesses reality through a mediation of nonutopian desire to become real; therefore, identifying architectural practices in the region is fundamental as they inform the critical analytical approaches. The following

2. See Liane Lefaivre, "Dirty Realism in European Architecture Today: Making the Stone Stony," *Design Book Review* 17 (Winter 1989); Liane Lefaivre, "Dirty Realism in der Architektur," *Archithese* 20, no. 1 (January/February 1990): 14–21.

3. This concept was used by Wouter Vanstiphout as an elegy for the postplanned city, which would have freed architecture from ideological determinisms, leading it to a "fight for little bits of reality." The main difference between Vanstiphout's dirty minimalism and the one described here is that while he welcomes the loss of planning and hierarchy with optimism, in our case, it is seen with dismay, so the abstract architecture produced by this current is first and foremost a will to resist and oppose the reality of the city. See Wouter Vanstiphout, "Dirty Minimalism: The Liberation of Unimportance in Recent Dutch Architecture," *Harvard Design Magazine* 24 (Spring/Summer 2006).

categories can help us classify the current production. They are not inert categories; in fact, they work better when overlapped and through constant interaction.

Dirty Minimalism:[3] Inspired by a strong modernist heritage, this style revives the brutalist language of the 1960s and 1970s through simplified forms and smooth surfaces. It is dirty because it moves from the pristine architectural object toward a self-mediated understanding of its context, operating through incursions into reality. Examples include adamo-faiden (Argentina), Barclay & Crousse (Peru), Metro Arquitetos (Brazil), and Pezo von Ellrichshausen (Chile).

Architectural Activism: A socially engaged practice that sees architecture as a form of social action, often organized collectively, and with ecological sensitivity, using local materials and techniques. It holds a certain formal detachment and is greatly informed by the limitations and possibilities of the construction site. It understands architecture as a strategical possibility for action. It is exemplified by the practices of Al Borde (Ecuador), Estúdio Flume (Brazil), PLAN: B (Colombia), and AGA estudio (Venezuela).

Material Architecture: This approach is grounded in material poetics and aims for simplicity in form, intense material research, and an artisanal approach to construction. The material operations can range from more ornamental textured surface applications to structures built from architectural elements and their assemblies, for example, the brick, as in the works of José Cubilla (Paraguay), Carla Juaçaba (Brazil), Nicolás Campodonico (Argentina), and Matias Zegers (Chile).

As in these design practices, criticism also closely adheres to antimonumentality, favoring themes and objects of a smaller scale. The immediate proximity, within reach, becomes a shy yet still alive will to build from the trenches. Utopia gives way to a deontology of small redemptive actions, of what can be done when almost all optimism has faded. Nonetheless, a hesitant optimism moves forward, for within this theoretical-critical-projectual modesty, the beauty of small gestures flourishes. The critique presented here draws its essence from the critical contents of reality.

This section of *Log* thus seeks to re-present the South to the North, to interweave people and places. Our map spins the old Torres-García map to present an apparent normality, a return to what was before. But there is no return. In Mark Twain fashion, this region abandons the original point of departure, only to look back from a different perspective and,

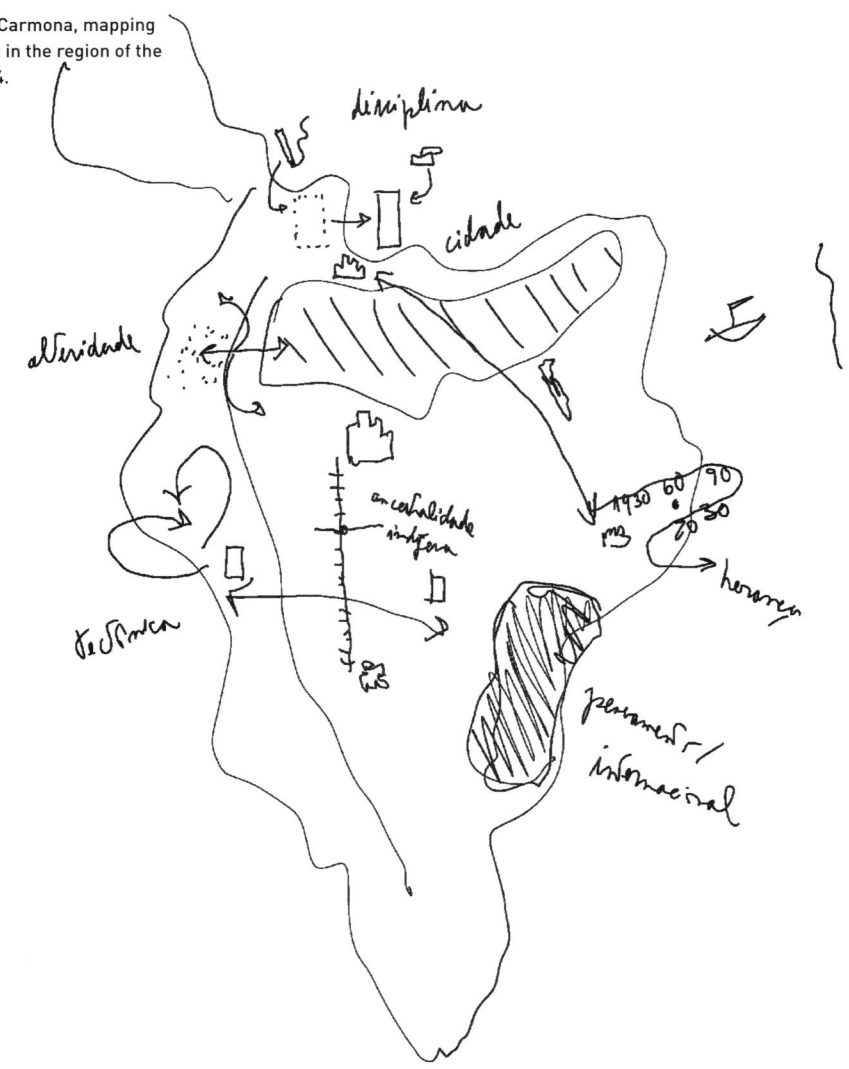

Jaime Solares Carmona, mapping critical thought in the region of the Far South, 2024.

Jaime Solares Carmona, a Brazilian architect and urban planner, is a PhD student at Yale. Previously a teacher at the Escola da Cidade in São Paulo, in 2023, he was named associate director of communications of the International Committee of Architecture Critics (CICA). He has published in *ArchDaily* and other periodicals and contributed to the books *Architecture as Built Criticism* (2024) and *Arquitetura Bicha* (forthcoming, 2025).

by this, decipher itself. I drew this map while I was still trying to understand how to connect such disparate social and cultural realities that, at first glance, presented exceptional critical vigor. So, I empirically resolved to understand reality on its own terms. I pieced together this map, which clarifies that critical thought in the region, although fragmented, presents some coherence, stemming from the possibility to operate its own dispersion in a transnational and transtemporal way. Each critic writes about their own place but also that of others. This critical collage offers us the possibility of overlays, indicating the nerve points of *this* America. After all, perhaps this disconnected cohesion is the only way to deal with the complexity and diversity that the region, and the world, presents.

Marina Waisman

Center, Periphery, and Region

Marina Waisman (Argentina, 1920–1997) was one of the 20th century's most influential Latin American historians, critics, and theorists. A defining feature of her thought is her avoidance of insularity and her consistent critical analysis of modern and postmodern culture without automatic adherence to imported agendas or a conservative reaction against them. Barcelona architect and writer Josep Montaner calls this approach "positive transculturation." Waisman's criticism represents an openness to the international debates that characterize modern and contemporary architectural thinking in Argentina. This phenomenon can also be seen in the influx of prominent architectural thinkers in the United States, including Diana Agrest, Mario Gandelsonas, Emilio Ambasz, Florencia Pita, and Hernán Díaz Alonso.

In 1985, Waisman founded and led the Seminarios de Arquitectura Latinoamericana (SAL), the most important forum for discussion of modernity, heritage, and regionalism in Latin America in the 1980s and 1990s. But it was her teaching, alongside her fruitful work as editor of *Summarios* (1976–1990), that produced many of the texts that are compiled in *El Interior de la Historia: Historiografía arquitectónica para uso de latinoamericanos* (The Inside of History: Architectural Historiography for the Use of Latin Americans), published in 1990 by Editora Escala, in Bogota, Colombia.

The following is the first English translation of the fourth chapter in the second part of that book, where, after laying the foundations of her historiography, Waisman weaves together a theoretical project for Latin America. She criticizes the binaries of center-periphery and center-margin as detrimental to the idea of the region and takes on Kenneth Frampton's concept of critical regionalism, countering his "resistance" agenda with the idea of "divergence" and recovering a potential future for local architecture. With this, she replaces some of the heroic and exoticizing tone of critical regionalism and suggests a subtle adherence to modernism (in her words, a "new modernism without adjectives") that produces a universality that neither exhausts the differences nor imposes colonial hierarchies. – *Jaime Solares Carmona*

The issue of the relationship between center and periphery far exceeds the cultural-economic-political issue that appears more directly linked to architectural problems, an issue that is barely the tip of an iceberg that penetrates deeply into historical reality. At present, the loss of the value of the center as a foundation, the sliding of the center toward the margins, and, as a consequence, the margins' acquisition of a particular central condition, could be considered the most characteristic features of this relationship.

At the risk of committing the sin that some philosophers attribute to architects – that is, the sin of dealing with philosophical concepts at a superficial level of analogies rather than their true meanings – I would like to make some references to philosophical orientations concerning the subject at hand, which can contribute to its more profound understanding, and for which I will mainly follow the exposition of Gianni Vattimo.[1] Vattimo examines the concept of nihilism derived from the philosophies of Nietzsche and Heidegger, who point out the coincidence of the crisis of humanism with the abandonment of the center on the part of Being. Being "dissolves its presence-absence into the network offered by a society increasingly transformed into an extremely sensitive organism of communication."[2] Nihilism is "the situation in which 'man rolls from the center toward X.'"[3] According to Nietzsche, the root of this nihilism lies in the loss of foundations, the "emphasis on the superfluity of the highest values," which ultimately represents the death of God.[4] To this loss of centrality of Being and to the abandonment of fundamental values, "the usual reaction is one which makes a grandiose metaphysical appeal to other, 'truer' values (for example, the values of subcultures or popular cultures as opposed to dominant cultures, the rejection of literary or artistic canons, etc.)."[5]

The great processes of destruction of artistic, architectural, and urban models carried out so far this century, first by the historical avant-gardes and then by the critical movement against modernism in architecture and urbanism, would find their framework in these statements.

A similar shift is also produced in art. According to Yves Michaud, "A large number of the most influential manifestations of contemporary art may consist precisely in the fact of shifting toward the centre . . . which usually remains at its margins."[6] But art itself, according to Heidegger, would also have a decorative and "marginal" essence:[7] its role would consist of creating a background rather than a "strong" subject since it has become the object of a "distracted perception."

1. Gianni Vattimo, *The End of Modernity: Nihilism and Hermeneutics in Post-modern Culture* (Baltimore: John Hopkins University Press, 1988).
2. Ibid., 47.
3. Friedrich Nietzsche, cited in Vattimo, 19.
4. Vattimo, 23–24.
5. Ibid., 25.
6. Yves Michaud, cited in Vattimo, 84.
7. Vattimo, 85.

I will add here another process of weakening of the center, which concerns the urban. Indeed, most of the world's large cities have been suffering, for several decades, from a process of "decentering" (a theme that some deconstructivist architects recognize as characteristic of their architecture). The major communal functions of the city, those that gave each city its particular character, are dispersed, they abandon the center, creating a diversity of subcenters, or "centers on the margins," which, for the same reason, cease to be strictly margins and themselves become centers, albeit "weak" centers because they no longer embody the overall sense of the city: the *Being* of the city. It could be said, then, paraphrasing the philosophical statements cited, that the Being of the city leaves the center and heads to X. This is not the place to elucidate the causes of such displacements, in which a transformation that reaches the most diverse structures of urban society is present. I will limit myself to mentioning it as one element of the general decentralization we are examining.

Now, this apparently apprehensible process, which can be related to postmodern society, is surely more complex and ambiguous than what is presented here. It is enough to consider the operation of "centralization of the margins" that Jorge Luis Borges carried out in the 1920s at the dawn of modernism. There was then a "peripheral" avant-garde in Buenos Aires, which drove the poetic structures of modernity, "moving the margin to the center of the Argentine cultural system," as Beatriz Sarlo explains in analyzing the poetic movements of the '20s and '30s.[8] In Borges's case, she points out the ability to raise the margins to the level of universality.

It is also worth remembering here that, even in 1929, José Ortega y Gasset devalued the notion of the center by asserting that Europeans considering themselves to be the center of the world is a sign of provincialism.[9]

In any case, in the present period, this situation of decentralization seems to have been assumed in a more general way, and thus from the "marginal" end of the center-margin relationship, it is up to us to decipher the counterparts of the center's loss of strength.

First and foremost, the consequent acquisition of some centrality by the margins is weak centrality because it is not universally valid and because its foundations are historical and existential, that is, changing and perishable. But it is centrality nonetheless.

It is also noted that the crisis of the models of the center has given rise to pluralism, has put an end to the cultural

8. Beatriz Sarlo, *Una Modernidad Periférica, Buenos Aires 1920–1930* (Buenos Aires: Ediciones Nueva Visión, 1988), 103.
9. José Ortega y Gasset, "Los 'ámbitos culturales,'" in *Las Atlántidas* (Madrid: Revista de Occidente, 1924).

Eladio Dieste, Iglesia de Altántida, Uruguay, 1960. From the original publication of this essay in *El Interior de la Historia*.

10. Two important examples can be cited in this regard: Severiano Porto in Brazil and Edward Rojas in Chile. In both cases, the architects formulate their own proposals based on the study of the local culture and environment. Porto's greater design maturity allows him to achieve, without difficulty, an original modern architecture without folkloric morphological bad habits, while Rojas is forging a difficult yet positive path in the same direction.

monopoly of the great countries of the West, and has thus sanctioned the legitimization of various local projects, including the decentralization of modeling – a possibility not always taken advantage of by local actors.

As the center maintained its strength, the peoples of Latin America necessarily appeared as marginal in architecture's cultural-production system. An undeclared but accepted scale of values placed – and to a large extent still places – the productions of certain countries considered central on the highest plane, a scale that is affirmed and prolonged thanks to the disciple-like attitude assumed by the majority of Latin American producers. But the displacements are beginning to be reflected in architectural production in both the theoretical and practical fields.

The process of raising awareness of cultural dependence on the part of formerly colonized peoples and the consequent affirmation of their own values have already been commented on. In the field of architecture, the instruments are being forged to explore reality in search of their own values. A few conspicuous examples point to possible orientations. The work of Hassan Fathy in Egypt, of B.V. Doshi or Charles Correa in India, and of the Latin Americans Rogelio Salmona, Severiano Porto, and Eladio Dieste, among others, ensures that there are possible and fruitful paths for such explorations.

The difficulties faced are not few: in architectural cultures inserted in a tradition of discontinuities, ruptures, and the constant irruptions of foreign ideas in local development, it is not easy to define one's own identity. History has recently been re-sorted. A new and widespread attraction for knowing one's own history has opened a way of reflection rarely found in this milieu – with the exception, of course, of historians. However, the passage from knowledge of history to the discovery of values that can be considered one's own, and then to the elaboration of guidelines for design based on these values, requires a series of conditions that go beyond research or theory and directly engage the quality – and the craft – of the designer.[10] (The present study aims precisely to highlight patterns of evaluation that can contribute to orienting architectural praxis toward the consolidation – or elaboration – of a regional identity).

Despite all of these shifts, the attraction of architectural production from central countries still predominates in local cultures, and it can perhaps be said that, to some extent, the reactions take place on the margins of the margins. The fact is that the center-margin relationship is marked, in this era

Severiano Porto and Mario Emilio Ribeiro, Posada en la Isla de Silves, Amazonia, Brazil, 1979. From the original publication of this essay in *El Interior de la Historia*.

of hypercommunication, not only by the conformation of the global system of production and consumption of goods – which has led certain sectors of both international and local communities to accept the passive role of consuming sophisticated products and of producing only the most basic ones – but also by the intrinsic power of information, more potent in terms of its "weak" status compared to systems of political or economic domination.

Much more intensely than in the past, this circumstance places different cultures at the crossroad between *universalism* and *localism*, or regionalism, between the universal and the particular, between the need to move to the general rhythm of the world and, at the same time, to remain true to themselves. The great architectures of the past were by no means immune to the weight of the great universal movements and even of the most direct transculturations. Gothic, Renaissance, and mannerist architecture spread from well-defined centers to the most distant regions, acquiring their own characteristics, the product of assimilating to a way of doing or a way of seeing corresponding to their new locale and sometimes becoming symbolic expressions of the new nationality – such was the case of the Gothic in England. The dissemination of ideologies, methods, procedures, images, and linguistic forms has always been an essential element of the historical fabric.

However, the conditions of that dissemination have changed radically in the contemporary world, and so have the power relations between the world's nations. From the period when the masters of the Gothic carried their ways of making architecture from one country to another, to when the treatise writers disseminated the Renaissance or mannerist models to the most distant countries, up to the present situation, the magnitude of the quantitative changes that have occurred in the processes of cultural dissemination has produced a fundamental qualitative alteration. The acceleration of history and of changes in social life, in expectations, in ways of life; the multiplication and new reach of media, which have eliminated distances and cultural differences in terms of the reception of information; the mechanisms of consumer society, which encourage a constant renewal of objects and forms, decreeing obsolescence and proclaiming new values that, in turn, will fall under the law of consumption, have all resulted in the creative, positive, and enriching character of cultural dissemination. This is, however, often submerged under the negative aspects of a passive and superficial acceptance, by which new forms are superimposed on existing cultural forms without entering into close connection with them, but rather simply replacing them and interrupting their possible development.

Another perverse effect of the power of information is the reductionism that operates in the transmission of architecture and, ultimately, in architecture itself. The media, with its magnificent graphic quality, reduces built architecture to a representation trimmed of all of its context, two-dimensional, eloquent in the impact of its images, which are often "constructed" by a skilled photographer. Such a reductive operation assigns the appreciation of architecture to only one of the senses, that of sight, leaving aside its spatial, material, sound, and environmental richness. At the same time, this way of evaluating architecture has encouraged more than one professional to conceive of their work in "photogenic" terms, looking for effects that may be irrelevant in the built work but that could enhance its presence on the printed page. This may be one of the causes of the conceptual impoverishment and constructive schematism of much of today's architecture.

The imbalance that exists between the quality and quantity of information emitted and disseminated by the central and "peripheral" countries is also a perverse effect, causing disinformation rather than information. Lack of communication blocks the exchange of information between marginal countries, a blockade that developed for complex reasons, among them the persistence of a communications system typical of the colonial world in which, after almost two centuries of political independence for Latin American countries, relations between former colonies and colonizers continue to be privileged while the exchange among colonies is hindered.

The information system thus serves to feed the mechanisms of consumption – consumption of information, and thus the consumption of languages, images, and ideas – supported by the periphery's acceptance of products endorsed by tradition, power, and prestige and their counterpart: the disinterestedness of those who come from the world considered peripheral and lacking those attributes. However, I have already alluded to the movement that aspires to reverse this process, a movement that is gaining strength year after year.[11]

The conflict between universalism and localism, between adherence to the central models that appropriate for themselves the condition of universality and the formulation of specific models, seems to recognize the aforementioned relationship between reflection and praxis as the core of the problem.[12] This relationship appears to be broken in the case of marginal countries. In effect, their roots and their insertion

11. Suffice it to mention the numerous meetings, architecture biennials, congresses, symposia, etc., that are held regularly in various Latin American countries; the meetings of architecture magazines, which try to intensify mutual knowledge, the first step toward the consolidation of the so-called Latin American unity; and in particular, the now institutionalized SAL seminars, which began in 1985 and consist of days of reflection and debate between architects and critics, aimed at guiding Latin American architecture toward the consolidation of its own identity.
12. See the chapter "Reflexión y Praxis" in *El Interior de la Historia.*

in a given physical and cultural reality are lost when systems are transferred to new mediums. Architectural ideologies, when they are transferred, instead of appearing as the result of complex debates around proposals and solutions, instead of exhibiting the polemic character between their ideas and achievements, are presented (or received) as *closed systems*, as great conceptual schemes of universal and definitive value. What's more, they lose their essential character as a *step in a process* – a theory/praxis/critique/reformulation of theory – and appear as a final and irrefutable phase of reflection. As long as an architectural theory remains open to dialogue with historical reality, it will continue to generate valid concepts and instruments to operate in that reality, but when that dialogue is broken, it becomes impotent, incapable of renewing itself or of acting productively in reality.

Thus these theories or ideologies that are transformed, at best, into more or less rigid conceptual schemes or, more frequently, into a mere collection of images enter a new reality that has certainly not participated in its elaboration. If this new medium has a more or less solid architectural tradition, the new ideas will probably be confronted with the body of concepts or the existing modes of production. In this encounter, there will be an exciting exchange, and orientations will be generated that verify the necessary balance between the movement of universal thought and the particularities of local culture.

But if, as has happened in most of the countries peripheral to the centers of power, there is no tradition of architectural thought or a sufficiently grounded degree of self-consciousness, it is most likely that the transplanted system of ideas will remain alien to the local reality, that it will not be deeply incorporated – that is, it will not put down new roots. Its own alienated condition will, in turn, lead to a process of further alienation from the culture on which it imposes itself by the force of its prestige, the alienation between reflection and praxis, and the alienation between praxis and the cultural and social environment. Even the issues proposed for reflection frequently repeat, without significant variations, as the issues and modes of reflection from the country of origin;[13] praxis will often accept procedures or images coming from the reflection and praxis of others. Interiority loses an opportunity to consolidate or strengthen itself and is snatched away into pure exteriority. This "Being" will also have left its center toward X…

In this way, for Latin American countries, with their sometimes hesitant or insufficiently defined cultural consciousness

13. Such was the case with the exercises on urban areas developed in a group of studies in Buenos Aires at the end of the 1970s (called "La Escuelita"), evidently influenced by contemporary European theoretical proposals.

and feeling of constituting the periphery in the Western world, the transfer of architectural ideologies becomes, all too often, one of the many processes of alienation that they suffer daily in the social, economic, or political fields.

These questions, as expected, were noted in our countries before they were in Europe.[14] However, for some time now, some international critics have been considering *regionalism* as a positive trend in architecture that reinforces or maintains regional identities and as a constructive opposition to various negative forms of universalism. The term *regionalism*, however, is extremely ambiguous because it can refer to positions that fluctuate between both local reinterpretation of international ideas and reactionary conservatism of a folkloric or populist nature. It seems, therefore, indispensable to pull out elements for a definition that makes an instrumental use of the term possible, removing it from the terrain of vaguely nostalgic aspirations.[15] One aspect to be considered in this definition is the discussion of the terms in use, a topic that I will return to shortly.

One of the elements that can effectively contribute to the formation of architecture in a regional sense is the analysis of the role and character of technology and its relationship with the concept of modernity. In fact, it seems accepted that architecture's degree of "progress," or modernity, should be measured by its access to advanced technology, the so-called high tech. In a recent interview, Oriol Bohigas argued that it is not a question of basing one's identity on underdevelopment or poverty but on the struggle to achieve the technology of development.[16] Now, what should be understood in our countries by advanced technology? The graceful and monumental constructions of Norman Foster or of Helmut Jahn, the fabulous domes of Buckminster Fuller, the subtle skins of César Pelli or of Kevin Roche?

The strength of the ideas – and propaganda – of the developed world, based on the ideology of modernity, has led us to take for granted that the only path to progress is the one that these countries followed – accepting that concept of progress as fact. We try to follow it – each time getting further and further away – even after its disastrous sequences for the stability of the world have become evident. Therefore, defining what "advanced technology" means for our countries seems urgent. In a first approximation, it could be said that advanced technology is that which allows, based on human resources and available materials and through its improvement and development, the achievement of the

14. Several years ago, I unsuccessfully tried to introduce a regional point of view at CICA (International Committee of Architectural Critics) by proposing a specific consideration for Latin American productions. More recently (1983), at a seminar organized by the Menéndez y Pelayo University in Santander, Spain, Ramón Gutiérrez, Antonio Toca, and I based our exhibitions on the values of regionalism, which was received with total disagreement among Spanish scholars. However, a few years later, the excellent Madrid-based magazine *Arquitectura Viva*, directed by one of these scholars, Luis Fernández-Galiano, accepted the regional criterion and has devoted articles and special issues to the subject.
15. Much progress has already been made in the theoretical field in this regard. Suffice it to cite the work of Enrique Browne and various articles by Silvia Arango and Cristián Fernández-Cox, in which a possible and desirable modernity is characterized for these countries. In the works presented to the various SALs, there can also be found important theoretical and practical material on the subject.
16. Interview with Oriol Bohigas, *Summa* 228 (August 1986).

highest degree of productivity to attain a habitat suitable for each region and way of life, both in quality and quantity.

It can be said that all materials are universal, both modern and ancient. But each of them, from brick to concrete, from wood to steel, has qualities and conditions in its production process and in its "process of use" that make it more suitable in different places. In Argentina, for example, the regional imbalance means that a technology acceptable for Buenos Aires becomes a caricature when used in semirural areas and, vice versa, that the transplantation of rural technologies and images is incoherent and anachronistic in the urban environment of the metropolis. As for the development of highly technical systems, this requires both a stable foreign policy and a strong internal market with permanent action, both conditions that are usual in only a few of our countries.

The use of regional resources does not imply stagnation or backwardness: among others, this is brilliantly proved by Eladio Dieste, Rogelio Salmona, and Togo Díaz as well as Severiano Porto, creator of an architecture of great value based on wood technology. The investigation of the qualities of regional materials, their adaptability to current needs, their response to environmental conditions, and the existence of a workforce with the capacity to develop and adapt to the necessary technical advances is one of the aspects to be emphasized in this search for regional identity.

So far, I have used the terms *center-periphery* and *center-margins* without examination. However, these terms are loaded with connotations that require careful debate.

In the first place, the center-periphery pair of concepts entails the idea of *dependence* because both terms belong to a system in which the second is subordinate to the first, occupying a secondary and accessory place. Everything that is produced in the periphery will be done within the framework of decisions made by the center. In the periphery, only "second-degree" decisions will be possible – which is to say, decisions taken within the framework created by the first-degree decision-making bodies. The models provided by the center will form the basis of all peripheral development, and in cases where these models cannot be reproduced, at least the image of the central model will be preserved as much as possible to indulge the picture provided by the center.

The acceptance of such a condition would require, on the one hand, that the condition responds effectively to a historically specific situation and, on the other, that it be decided to renounce any possibility of developing an architecture

17. Ramón Gutiérrez has analyzed this issue in various conferences. See *Summa* 251.

appropriate to the region. As for the former, a historical examination of Latin American architecture reveals that this has not been the type of relationship between colonizers and colonies in all periods. Ramón Gutiérrez[17] has pointed out that the complex origin of the Spanish models of Latin American colonial architecture reveals some unprecedented combinations in the center-country, a new product distilled from memories, procedures, and images, in turn modified to adapt it to the new domains with their different technological possibilities, and different urban or rural environments, so that the final result can hardly be inscribed in a model-reproduction relationship. In our century, the diversity of sources and the indiscriminate arrival of information make it generally difficult to recognize the possible models that have been the object of syncretic operations, almost never of literal repetitions. Perhaps it was only during the period of eclecticism and academicism that a direct relationship between the center and periphery could be detected – even though free and fanciful interpretations of the central models abounded – with the importation of plans, materials, technology, craftsmen, etc.

This unequal relationship throughout history would suggest that architecture has represented, more than once, the possibility of eluding the total weight of the central power and minimizing the relationship of dependence.

Regarding the second point – that is, the possibility of developing an architecture specific to the region – it should be borne in mind that the center-periphery system establishes a scale of values of the center, which will serve to categorize both central and marginal products. Thus everything that is done or not done, everything that is thought of or not thought, will necessarily be read according to what is done or thought in the center. The producer from the periphery will be judged, in the best of cases, as a gifted student; at worst, as an ignorant person incapable of understanding the subtleties of central production; but more often, he will simply be ignored – the most derogatory mode of categorization – known (although not always acknowledged) only in his closest environment.

I have previously commented on how the organization of historical material by central historiography inescapably places Latin American production out of context: the value system apt for understanding the central architecture is not apt for understanding the peripheral, but no alternative system has been created for that purpose.

In this way, by introducing the production of these countries into the center-periphery system, the same fallacy is committed when one historical period is judged in terms of the values of another. (One paradigmatic example is the misunderstanding and contempt for baroque art provoked by neoclassical ideology.)

The concept of periphery thus implies a lack of knowledge of each culture's intrinsic centrality with respect to itself – a "weak" centrality, perhaps, as has been said, but necessary if one intends to reach an understanding of its production and character.

These considerations regarding the term *periphery* are valid without major changes for the term *margin*. Both mark positions subordinate to a center, with an extrinsic ownership that does not give them the right to participate or allow them the freedom to define their own development.

From these reflections, it seems necessary to replace the terms *periphery* and *margin* with something more appropriate both to the historical situation and to the projects for the future. Therefore, the concept of *region* tends to replace those mentioned in recent studies. For the idea of region, unlike that of the periphery, locates each culture in a system that is based precisely on the plurality of regions, a system in which none of them exercises hegemony and cannot, therefore, be held up as a model of universal validity. In this system, the loss of the center that the philosophers cited above and the evaluation of "marginal" cultures in the absence of central values are evident.

The (totalitarian) idea of high culture is replaced, here, by that of cultural *pluralism*. The judgments about advantages or disadvantages that each culture presents in the various fields may enter into other systems – that of demography, climatology, agricultural or industrial production, etc. – within which they may be categorized according to their respective advantages or disadvantages, but they will not be value judgments that qualify or globally disqualify one regional culture over another. In this system, it is not necessary to place the production of a region on the Procrustean bed, to be shaped by the guidelines of the "central" countries until it qualifies. Instead, judgment is directed toward its own center, and in doing so, values can be distinguished that perhaps had not been discovered along with disvalues that had been confused in their deeper meaning.

The substitution of the concepts of periphery or margin by that of the region, the radical displacement of the point of

18. In this regard, the analysis of Silvia Arango may be cited with respect to the postmodern qualities of Latin American architecture of the 1940s; the studies by Ruth Verde Zein on Brazilian architecture after Brasília; the works of Eduardo Días Comas on the meaning of Lúcio Costa's work.
19. The theoretical work of Cristián Fernández-Cox deserves to be mentioned in this regard. See *Summarios* 126.

Marina Waisman was an architect, critic, and writer based in Buenos Aires. Special thanks to Diego Bari Waisman for authorizing this translation of her text from the Spanish and to Professor Ruth Verde Zein and Eloah Maria Coelho Rosa from Mackenzie Presbyterian University for sharing the research results of "Os Summarios de Waisman" in advance.

view – almost a Copernican revolution – has allowed architects, critics, and historians to direct a fresh, more constructive, and original look into their own history, relocating episodes in a new historiography,[18] as well as a look into an architectural praxis, laying the foundations of a theory.[19]

The regionalist approach can thus be accepted as a way of understanding the local circumstance in its most diverse aspects – ways of life, building traditions, and technologies, old and recent, urban images, typologies, etc. – without implying a limit within a narrow localism or freezing historical development, but as a way of consolidating and building a cultural world based on one's own model.

This "centralization" of cultures previously considered marginal can be interpreted in different ways: Kenneth Frampton, who has contributed greatly to bringing the issue to the table for international debate, sees it as a possibility of *resistance* to the apparatus of the postindustrial world, as a way of maintaining a vital nucleus without allowing oneself to be absorbed by the apparatus. I, for one, prefer to interpret it as a *divergence* within the general direction of postmodern culture, as an attempt to find alternative paths to those marked by global society.

The first would be a, so to speak, static interpretation: it is a matter of conserving something, of entrenching oneself in the face of the invasion of an undesirable system; it is a somewhat romantic or nostalgic position. The second, on the contrary, is a dynamic interpretation. It aims to express a project: given the restrictions that the apparatus of postmodernity presents to peripheral peoples in order to approach the central models, this line is abandoned in search of more appropriate – and possible – models for the fulfillment of their historical trajectory.

To resist is to preserve a situation, to create an enclave within the system so as not to be absorbed by it (but for how long?).

To diverge is to leave the system, to put aside its structures, to embark in unknown directions.

To resist is to remain so as to defend what one is.

To diverge is to develop, to break from what you are, and enable what you can become. Probably, the difference between these two interpretations comes from the difference in origin of their supporters: from the center, the margins cannot be seen as generators of projects but only, perhaps, as refuges. From the margins, everything is – or should be – a project.

Sérgio Ferro
Translated from the Portuguese
by Ellen Heyward

New Architecture

Editor's note: This essay is from
Architecture from Below: An
Anthology *(London: MACK,*
2024), the first of three planned
volumes of Sérgio Ferro's key
texts. Edited by Silke Kapp and
Mariana Moura, the trans-
lations were organized by
the joint Brazil/UK work-
ing group Translating Ferro
/ Transforming Knowledges
for Architecture, Design and
Labour for the New Field of
Production Studies (TF /
TK). Created in 2020, TF /
TK brought together more than
50 scholars worldwide to define
Production Studies, based on
and informed by Ferro's work.
Special thanks to Professor Silke
Kapp for making this publica-
tion possible.

Only three years after the 1964 military coup in Brazil, architect, historian, and theorist Sérgio Ferro wrote this essay as a
critique of his generation's architectural production. Many
years later, the essay's title would identify the thinking and
practice of Arquitetura Nova, a group led by Ferro, Rodrigo
Lefèvre, and Flávio Império. Ferro analyzes architecture from
the perspective of the construction site and the construction
process, a view that stands out from other historical materi-
alist approaches, which often lead the discipline to dead ends.
In contrast, Ferro's critical framework is forward-looking,
actively exploring the social possibilities that architecture
could embody. His critique of a post-Brasília (1960) architecture lays bare the contradictions between aesthetic form and
social content, a tension that intensified under the dictatorship
and later reemerged as a tragic paradox in neomodern contemporary Brazilian architecture.

The term *caboclo brutalism*, which describes an architecture
that has shifted from rawness to compensation, captures this
tension. Although Ferro uses it in a derogatory sense, there is a
sense of melancholy for what could have been rather than an
outright rejection of its aesthetic and ethical underpinnings. In
a later interview, Ferro explains that, despite its flaws, caboclo
brutalism, best represented in Paulo Mendes da Rocha's work,
retains the ethical foundation of European and Japanese brutalism. But the "constant repetition of exaggerated proposals,"
stemming from what Ferro understands as a "delusional rationality" of caboclo brutalism, is perpetuated by new generations
of the "São Paulo School," which make this ethical basis more
and more fraught. The escapist, self-centered, and self-iso-
lated architecture that he describes will devolve into cynicism
in the 1990s. Ferro's analysis enables us to trace the origins of
this school of thought. By encouraging a deeper understanding
of the relationship between ethics and aesthetics in Brazilian
architecture, he opens a space for dialogue about architectural
production on the periphery of global capitalism. This common
condition across many Global South countries is particularly
relevant to understanding many Latin American architectural
theories and practices today. — *Jaime Solares Carmona*

1. Although the Brazilian Portuguese word *projeto* is usually equivalent to the English *design*, the stress here lies on its connotation as a prospect, a plan for the future – that is, a project.

A completed work of architecture both hides and reveals a project;[1] and like anything executed in practice, it deforms – attenuating or altering – its initial proposal, nevertheless sticking to the basic guidelines. A work of architecture therefore enables us to reconstitute quite accurately the most significant features of that project's structure.

The project, in architecture, involves various different levels. It is a specific solution to an immediate problem, and it is a reflection of the author's general stance, and thus of the times in which they live. By closely observing and analyzing a finished piece of architecture, and by scrutinizing the consistencies and inconsistencies among its parts and levels, the deeper intentions and attitudes of its design can be pinpointed. Objective contradictions in an architectural work – such as in its construction process, its use, the reactions it provokes, or the instruments employed to build it – end up rendering explicit internal gaps and incoherences between the specific design and the general attitude that justifies and informs it.

The project, both in the specific sense and as a reflection of a general attitude, is the intentional articulation of the field of possibilities that a given situation yields. In architecture, the field that must be articulated has limits – such as the available technical standard or a rather strict building program – and a realm of freer options, which do not depend on immediate determinations and are therefore better equipped to express ideological fluctuations from moment to moment. For example: the small number of structural types available at any given time still enables several forms of usage. Although a supporting structure itself serves as a clear index of the technical stage we might have reached in building construction, each and every choice we make along its selection and design process expresses our needs, inclinations, and expectations. And over time, the variations in our choices and designs not only follow a technical evolution (often nonexistent) but also the variations in the broader social context and its impact on each of us.

If we direct our attention to such subtle shifts when examining the projects coming from the new generation of Brazilian architects, and in particular from those of a rational orientation based in São Paulo, we may notice some common features. In short, theirs are proposals designed for an anticipated development that, in an inversion of functions, progressively turn into compensatory measures for their growing frustrations. The inversion is achieved by fictitiously isolating an architectural object, thereby pretending to render concrete the intended development inside the object's microcosm.

During the military coup d'état on March 31–April 1, 1964, the Brazilian Army assembled vehicles near the National Congress of Brazil, in Brasília.

The aggressive and provocative attitude toward the prevailing reality that produced these proposals is gently replaced by gestures of a substitutive, conciliatory representation.

Any piece of proactive and responsible modern architecture makes proposals that cater to longed-for progress and collective needs – this is normal for an activity whose nucleus (design) always implies a future that is to be built collectively. From Ledoux to Le Corbusier, there is no shortage of forward-thinking suggestions, and they matter more than the simple functionalism of any rigorous, well-behaved observance of a mostly imposed building program. Such hypothetical foresights, besides displaying the kind of development intended, end up accusing their most painstaking limitations by contradicting the very present that stokes them.

Rare are the proposals that actually come to fruition, or whose fruition occurs as originally intended. The difference between the proposal and its fruition is directly proportional to the distance in which the longed-for future becomes visible: the greater the distance, the more fantastical the forecast and, therefore, the more convenient the appropriations. There have been moments, however, such as in Brazil between 1940 and 1960, when the symptoms of a probable social development – false or otherwise, though believed to be real – stimulated optimistic forecasting. The future appeared to contain forthcoming promises, which hypothetically required new instruments. The proposals, supposedly capable of almost immediately coming to fruition, sought to attach themselves to the concrete availabilities in our particular context and to the deficiencies of our underdevelopment.

This is what distinguishes the work of Oscar Niemeyer and Vilanova Artigas: they put forward a sober, direct kind of architecture, armed with all the appropriate resources for the Brazilian context, and equipped themselves with the clarity, openness, and constructive courage befitting vaguely announced transformations. Brasília heralded both the culmination and the interruption of these hopes: shortly after, we halted our timid, illusory social progress and heeded the military curfew.

When the current crisis began around 1960, young architects, steeped in a tradition whose driving concern was great collective need, felt the growing gap between the narrow scope of their professional tasks and their education and expectations. While their work was still focused on the same ends, the opportunities to execute their projects diminished and their prospects waned. Yet their proposals continued along much the same lines, with no need for particular addenda: in theory, the tools for organizing space for a new, more human time were ready, even if their preemptive nature only ever allowed for abstract formulations. The new architects repeated them. But being aware both that their proposals faced inevitable and immediate frustration and of the collapse of developmentalism, they were tainted with an increasing aggressiveness. It destroyed the balance and flexibility such proposals possessed as long as they were believed to be achievable. Architects at first reacted to the deferral of their hopes with a renewed, accentuated affirmation of their initial positions – forging the home-grown, hybrid *caboclo*[2] brutalism (as opposed to the overtly aesthetic European brutalism), the forced "didactification" of procedures, excessive constructive rationalization, and the "economism" that generated ultradense spaces rarely justified by objective impositions.

These architects, hot on the heels of mannerism, reflected a growing generalized discontent. Indeed, if we ignore the effects of this understandable aggressiveness, the architectural work completed during this phase displays an abuse of rigid petrification and schematization, which denounces the country's deepening structural decomposition. Just to reiterate: from 1960 onward, and in the case of projects from the most significant group of new architects, proposals that previously

2. *Caboclo* was a term used to identify persons with European and Indigenous ancestry, and thus a metonymy for something typically Brazilian. Nowadays it may be considered derogatory, although Ferro means it in a positive sense.

Paulo Mendes da Rocha and João de Gennaro, Casa no Butantã, São Paulo, Brazil, 1967. Photo: Nelson Kon. The images accompanying this translation have been added to Ferro's text. The projects are emblematic of the architectural production at the time of its writing.

characterized Brazilian architecture, and which were created for a once probable development, were reprised with exaggerated emphasis. This emphasis resulted from an awareness of these proposals' impracticability and the disappearance of their fragile social basis – signed, sealed, and delivered by the irrational interruption of our slow social process.

Yet this exaggeration has even more sources. Those proposals, despite having never been fully executed as originally intended, ended up serving different and even opposing goals. Previous research into urban planning or into our constructive limitations is today, after being conveniently deformed, employed by the very forces it once intended to change and challenge: dictatorship and imperialism. Planning is thus transformed from a means of optimizing resources into an instrument for imposing internal restrictions and subservience to the masters of more advanced technology (and of capital), with complete disregard for and violation of the Brazilian condition. This results in indigestion, as well as paralysis of any efforts made toward achieving an autonomous, appropriate development. It results in the opposite of the original intentions guiding that research. On the other hand, by carefully picking and choosing, the cultural industry (industrial sub-design, "specialized" magazines, and decorative or imitative architecture) and real estate speculation could revert any proposals that were not overly aggressive for their own benefit. The inexhaustible anthropophagic capacity of the commercially based system – reinforced by the propaganda of mostly superfluous commodities and a chronic dearth of stimulating novelties – easily swallowed that which appeared to contain the requisites of a modifying attitude; and Brazilian architecture, castrated, served as its sales agent.

What best demonstrates the concrete absurdity of the new architecture's key manifestations is the ongoing, voracious consumption of architectural language, permanently weakened in its aggressiveness by the spurious trivialization diluting its expressive force, combined with the curtailment of the professional field on account of the crisis. Increasingly confined to producing work for private sector clients (such as bourgeois residencies, shops, or clubs), architects are under dual pressure to make the most of the professional distortion – the private sale of collective knowledge – as an anguished, contradictory opportunity to insistently affirm their most generic theses. These isolated works of architecture are of petty self-importance, and by evading the direct control of the system, end up clinging to the most bitter contradictions of that very system. The shocking presence of general theses in the vacuously private nature of these works clearly demonstrates the impasse architects reach in practicing their profession: the very same project that affirms them also jeopardizes them.

The sum of these two adverse requests – one specific and private, the other theoretical and transformative – produces hybrid, disconnected constructions whose message gets tangled up in its own rhetoric. When this opposition – between what architects know and propose and what they are allowed to do – is not concealed but rather vehemently displayed in their constructions, it objectively assumes the characteristics of a complaint. But the distance between the awareness of one's capacity and one's insubstantial practice weighs heavily and taints their attempts. The complaint begins to show the signs of an insurmountable contradiction. Architects, impeded from taking the directions they should, experiment with surpassing this limitation by using the directions' forms to paint an outline. Alienated from their real function by an out-of-date system, they react from within the lane allocated to them by the system, thus deepening the breach between their work and the objective situation that must be fought. To confront the negative forces diluting them, they accept the fragmentation of the particularity of their specific designs, which is another form of dilution. Densifying their designs, coating them in elaborate conjuring tricks with which to attack, architects stray further and further from their object of aggression and from the very possibility of aggression: overly complex, they are no longer heard. In their attempts to dis-alienate themselves, they only amplify their own alienation. This is the limit of a critical attitude within architecture: the radicalization of contradiction stretched to absurdity. The situation is obviously insurmountable via architectural paths.

But oftentimes the entailing contradiction is almost unbearable. The certainty that their professional activity is absurd under these conditions, and that their reaction is naive, provokes discontent and insecurity among the new generation of architects. To escape it, they devise disguises to compensate for their initial frustration. Now, the very reaction process – an emphatic reprisal of previous positions at any given opportunity – provides the means of escape, with the added advantage of still appearing to be a reaction. In short, the available escape route is the following: the constant repetition of exaggerated proposals, which are now utopic and (therefore) scrawny, disaggregate the aggressive overall intention of broader development that structured them in the first place. And they disaggregate precisely due to the exaggerated nature of each part. Their form, once expanded, schematized and rhetoricated by didactic and combative efforts, has corrupted the economy of the old articulatory intention with its dynamic balance of what is and what ought to be. This undoes its essential significance, which resided precisely in the realist adaptations it made to the possibilities that were effective at the time. The forms for a given content are limited, and this content cannot resist infinite formal variations, especially when it is compromised by an opposing reality (the substantive rationality of previous proposals compromised by the irrational particularity of the specific commission, for example). After the guiding prospect has been dismantled, only the quasi-isolated proposals linger, and these are reorganizable solely when viewed as part of the contradictory position currently under examination. Less attentive observation will always see these remaining proposals as actually isolated, lacking any further justification and favoring immanentist interpretations – that is, interpretations that bow down to their supposed internal significance and truth. These proposals favor and facilitate the passage [from heroism to resignation], and any architects that abdicate a conscientious, responsible attitude – one that would require a dramatic sharpening of inevitable contradictions – quickly make this jump.

The (coerced and self-destructive) history of a progressive position and its language turns into a history of the evolution of a self-sufficient technique. The instruments of aggression, and of a phase in our hypertrophied development, acquire autonomy as truths in and of themselves. Moreover, history and instruments – transfigured in and fetishized as an internal evolution, and preserving the aura bestowed upon them by the coherence of the formerly aggressive attitude – appease whoever wishes to appear proactive but actually is not. In one fell swoop, they recover their ricocheted self-esteem and respect, as well as the comfort of harmless, nearly effortless "rationality." Planning, previously preached as rationality in amongst the Brazilian chaos, becomes the recipe for remedying any conspicuous disarray – particularly because, as it was only actually executed once before [in Brasília], it lends itself to ample and easy speculations. Whereas before the use of raw concrete, in all its rusticity, contributed to a more truthful and economic construction, today, for reasons nobody cares to analyze, it commands the fussiest of filigrees. Likewise, the new organization of floor plans and spaces – a result of attentive reasoning – led to the inconsequential exoticism of hyperbolic arrangements. And all this is explained by carefully analyzing the immanent signification of techniques and materials, protected by the very rationality of their evolution. The crystallized technical realm takes on an active role: it contains the truth. What used to be a tool becomes the motivation. It is enough to follow its path. The bad faith is evident: architects' increasingly gratuitous choices are now ascribed to the "being" of the architectural work, to its intrinsic nature. The comfortable transferal of responsibility is ready, hidden by a bastard filiation to the arduous conquests of the pioneering architects. What used to be aggression now serves as compensatory substitution. Not that these escapist architects settle for our present irrational situation. Rather they flee, docilely, instead of radicalizing their contradictions toward a collapse, or indeed acting in any capacity at all.

Examples of this inversion.

Supporting structures have always been a fundamental concern for Brazilian architects, and for various reasons: opposition to the primitivism of our antiquated methods of construction; a didactic need for a movement seeking affirmation; a reflection of an overall rationalizing view stimulated by the promise of development. Even if structures were chosen and afforded a certain excess, they met demands deriving from actual experiences. Today, however, the work of many architects from the new generation betrays a hemorrhaging of pseudo structures, regularly presenting a new design of the few formulas compatible with our limited possibilities – rarely suited to building programs' reduced dimensions. Artificially underlined to display their presence, distorted to flaunt more "logic" than they actually have, these structures

conceal several deformations. Compared to their predecessors, they immediately reveal their absurdity: simplicity and efficiency have been sidelined for the pleasure of individual virtuosity. But it is a superficial virtuosity, conditioned to the abolition of the structure's balance between being and appearing. Hiding necessary beams, sizing arbitrarily, reinforcing vaults as if they were slabs, overusing useless concrete panels, demonstrating deceitful sturdiness – these are essentially the main tools. Not that absolute rigor when it comes to mathematical calculations is required. But even poetic license has its limits. Without a doubt, these structures are more aggressive than their predecessors, partially accounting for the forced renovation of architectural language. However, this "didactification" of their reason for being (that is, of constructive rationality) becomes practically their only raison d'être – maligning their real rationale, which is to structure. They are transformed into a rational apparatus that is irrationally employed. The former substantive rationality is dismantled and, in absence of any new substantive rationality, slides into a deceitful, limited, gratuitous one.

The fact that these structures are interchangeable and often completely absurd – those familiar with design processes in architectural firms or competitions cannot deny it – does nothing to counter the illusion that they are based on a hypothetical truth immanent to the technical realm. On the contrary, irrationality is their direct consequence. This truth simply does not exist. Rather, the science of the resistance of materials exists; the calculation of structures exists. But what does not exist is the meaning or the value attributed to the structures themselves, supposedly justifying the truth projected upon them. A structure only acquires meaning or value when it is sustained by an authentic project – that is, by a general intention that impregnates the structure with meaning, and by its selection and articulation with the work's remaining elements, and with whatever is external to it.

As architects indulged in the fragmentation of once organically coherent proposals, a responsibility was transferred to the structures: the responsibility to define the meanings that their language (the one of their excessive proposals) may take on. Architects relinquished the conscious, creative act of selection and rearticulation intended to reveal experienced contradictions. Thus ensued the fantasy of individualized structures (or of any other element): if the meaning is inherent to the structures, then a structure whose meaning is compatible with the meaning of the building program must be sought – something that is also frequently reified.

Seeing as this meaning does not actually exist, only the architect's "sensitivity" serves as a guide. Obviously, when such sensitivity is satisfied, it is for other reasons. The impracticability of wishing for correlated meanings lies in the fact that there are no meanings to correlate. Since every act of perception is significant, including the perception of building structures, architects recognize in them a meaning that they themselves unconsciously set, but whose origin they attribute to the structure. And uncontrolled as the relation is, when this meaning satisfies desires, needs or anxieties, architects applaud the magnificent harmony of the monads and surrender themselves to the charms of emotional connections without paying attention to the surreptitious catharsis.

What disappears are the loaded options for and answers to reinforced concrete, the seriousness of a technology whose limited availability in the Brazilian context gave rise to its finest manifestation of active, conscious freedom. Unconsciousness disguises the guilty inconsistency of an attitude undone by illusionist gestures. In their fugue, the new generation of architects submits to the parasitic meanings they blindly attribute or receive through inertia – the effect is the same. Sensitivity, hereby hollow and vague, has nothing to do with an aesthetic approach to the architectural work. Architecture only possesses an aesthetic dimension when

Francisco Petracco and Pedro Paulo de Melo Saraiva, Clube XV, Santos, Brazil, 1964. © Arquivo F. Petracco.

a design's coherence is profoundly anchored in a practical commitment. That is, when a design responds, in technical terms, to the objective necessity that impels its existence. The aesthetic dimension is the recognition of the design's dense and authentic synthesis, or rather of the assisted articulation that proposes to amplify the situational information to the full extent of its possibilities. The aesthetic dimension is the result of the immense human implications that a technique might possess. Fetishized poor technique – the essence of the deformed structural abundance of many new generation designs – is the cloaked fear of responsibility, rather than aesthetic diligence.

Structure, in architecture, simultaneously provides a technical solution to an immediate problem and reflects an organized vision of the reality within which it is proposed. When the consciousness of the contradiction between actual opportunities and the potential of Brazilian architectural thinking is not clearly and critically objectified in architectural works, exaggerated structures become the almost exclusive artifice employed to establish a semblance of rational order in objects whose insignificance is widely recognized, such as the bourgeois residence.

The lack of a critical and aggressive stance has the aggravating effect of adorning, with a guise of rationality, the absurdity of the particularization imposed on architects' eminently social function. The ongoing nature of this procedure reveals that the detour also somehow serves the architects who wield it: through compensation. From the maniacal accentuation of ridiculous disguise to the anguished recognition of the unfeasibility of a coherent approach, within this misplaced aggressiveness or creativity, in spite of it all, these architects feel like they exist, like they are participating. The aggressive disguise compensates for their awareness of the vacuousness of their work. Curiously, we are witnessing, here, the renaissance of magical expectations.

In these cases, the architectural work resembles an inverted ex-voto, intending to obtain from itself, and for its author, the recommendation of an organized totality capable of mitigating the dearth of actual guiding prospects. In the absence of a clear vision of the situation, any type of order is aspired to, in the hopes of fleeing insecurity. The operation is markedly magic. If reality is confusing and overwhelming, instead of making an effort to understand it, the comfortable trend of simplified deformity as an internal act of will emerges; the vision is altered without altering that which is viewed. This arbitrary will adapts to any solution: the nature of the fictitious order is indifferent, as long as it is ordered. In the now formally hypostasized structures, the content of the old structures disappears; their materiality and adaptation are embroiled in the repetition of what they should be, while what they are clashes with this sought-after coherence. Masked structuralism, changing its attire by illusorily maintaining its principles, loses sight of the foundation of its former attitude and of its very basis, which depend on the interaction between the concrete fact – the work of architecture that must be structured here and now, with its present material content – and the possibilities of a compatible change. The result is a pantomime.

Another example.

Density – which once derived from a justifiable spatial economy in an underdeveloped country, deficient in constructions – invades all architectural work, including luxury buildings.

The minute logic of each function's detailed specification crams the space in myriad ways, almost all of which are dispensable. Nonetheless, if density is rarely motivated by concrete reasoning, we can once again presume that it fulfils other needs. In parallel to this abundant production of abnormally fussy details and subdetails are the signs of a morbid attitude: petrification into geometric shapes, abuse of concrete panels that artificially exhibit the marks of their step-by-step production process (the boards and slabs drawn one by one), increasingly violent textures, modular or free-form shredding of continuous surface areas – and all this definitively stratified and trying hard to demonstrate individuality. The reification of this unsolicited, analytical verbiage is only explicable via the same reasoning of any exaggerated structuralism: the urgency to elude its own emptying. As such, the potential complexity of a work of architecture concretely and intensely engaged with the whole of society is represented by the quantity of irrelevant minutiae, a caricature of complexity. The intimate relation of actual organic processes is exchanged for the mechanical adherence of multiplied and amorphous juxtapositions. It is the mastery of quantity that populates the fluid, sticky, and unstructured mental world of humans in the era of massification. Its alarming appearance stems precisely from the perennially latent awareness of its illusory, artificial nature. It stems from the ill temper and resentment of a known lie. And petrification attempts to stave off this awareness. Excessive coloration is always the counterweight to some basic lack; a flagged detour always corresponds to its opposite when it comes to human relations and productions. Petrification of quantity and false density hide the fact that today's architecture, if it is not critical, is nothing at all. Here, the paradox of the encounter of human movement with the opacity of matter – of which artworks are made – gives up its open-ended nature and loses its ephemeral balance: it remains, as though it were still human objectification, the absolute obtusity of the thing [reification]. It is a primary and final manner of affirmation of the status quo through the negation of one's own freedom and movement. Dense stone is the perfect model of the thing-in-itself: complete, blind, unchanging, indifferent, fulfilling the role of inexistent security – with the added distinction of bad faith and immense obtusity.

It is currently fashionable to see architecture as a system of signs.

It is undeniable that we are witnessing the transformation of all architectural elements, and of their ensemble, into signs of themselves. This is evidenced, precisely, by exaggerated and misplaced formal structuring, by density and petrification, and by countless other parallel aspects that shall remain unexamined here, such as functional schematization, guiding modules and grids, and the ever-excessive didacticism.

It is necessary, however, to make some distinctions here. First, it is convenient to separate sign and symbol. The sign results from the arbitrary addition of content to form. Symbols, on the other hand, are ways of participating. Their structure produces resonances that resemble those motivated by the symbolized content. But symbols are also forms of representation. They substitute the immediate presentation of the content to which they refer with their transposition in the realm of metaphor. In this sense, all artistic activity is a symbolizing activity (and architecture, in spite of everything, is still art, at least in the case of works of adequate significance). In the architecture of the new generation, the authentic symbol has disappeared. The desired content, being evermore distant, is not consolidated in any particular form, while externally symbolic forms merely shroud the frustration of the former prospects. If they are still symbols, it is only by virtue of inversion: they indicate the need for new content. But this inversion corrupts the very nature of the symbolic process, which is the apprehension of something existent, of content that is diffuse yet real. The inverse is propitiatory magic.

In truth, between us there are no symbols (the last one was the unfinished mandala of Brasilia Cathedral). There are conventional signs, extracted from the repertoire of industrialized productions – half correct, half fictional – and from former symbols, diluted and dismantled by the disappearance of the contents and needs that sustained them. And it could not be any other way: the symbol is always structural, and it is exactly this structural vision that is lacking.

The definition of architecture as "a language with self-reflexive structures, without semantic content and whose syntax is redefined in each case,"[3] the height of tautology stating that architecture is what it is, is really a matter of indicating the phenomenon of the introduction of signs into contemporary architectural objects – a specific experience, arbitrarily generalized to architecture as a whole. The refusal to accept the difficult concrete reality leads to glossing over any immediate evidence of the spurious use of architecture with an alienating, impalpable fog, suggestive of an alternative reality. It is the fog of falsifying signs and their trussed-up rationality that retains and discharges an inevitable dissatisfaction with the object and the society that produced it. For example, the actual absence of industrialized architecture – despite the fact that it would be possible and has already been tested and theoretically accepted – leads to the multiplication of details that might be typical of a system of prefabricated components, to the diversification and showcasing of functions that have no basis in the artisanal construction process, or to proposals for social programs in ultralimited situations. Locks, door frames, windowsills, and joints have the logic of rigorous abstraction, as if they were tests for later general application. Details are drawn as if they did not possess any obvious motivation – they are excessively explained in an effort to justify themselves. Architecture only dons signs that represent itself when, in order to forget what it is, it superimposes the image of what it ought to be.

Having lost its reason for being, today's architecture mocks its utopic potential. It knows it is not what it pretends to be, and it underlines what it knows it is not. Its aborted project displays the markings of abortion. Architecture vaguely indicates what it could be if it were able to develop itself, but the truncated development only allows a monstrous promise. Architecture plays a role: it is a comedian. It realizes it is an actor in a role that enthralls it, engages it and continuously eludes it. And, the more perfect the performance, the greater the frustration; when it sees itself performing, all the greater its frustration and rancor. And in attempting to overcome the frustration, this rancor leads to petrification,

3. Ferro quotes from his notes on a course taught by the Italian semiotician Umberto Eco in São Paulo around 1966. Eco's books that make reference to architecture, such as *La struttura assente* (1968), had not yet been published.

as if magically suppressing the distance between comedy and concretion. But seeing as the attempt is in bad faith, frustration and rancor reappear, and the cycle begins once more. Language is combined with metalanguage. While those who build within a concrete prospect are designing, it is only for a near future densely armed by the present. Those who design into the void, instead, see the future as unlikely, distant, utopian, and unachievable. To seek this future and to move away from the present, forms are strengthened with fictional characteristics. They invent to escape. Somewhat indifferently, they create the image of a future whose key requisite is to be something other than today. And accents are morbidly applied to accentuate such alterity. Vicious architecture projects virtues in order to virtuously shroud its own vices. However, the aspired envelopment is bound to what it envelopes, because it is the enveloped that yields the envelopment. Such architecture wishes to be judged on the basis of the image it creates for itself – disjunction, bad faith, compensation.

The understanding of architecture as a system of signs falsely generalizes a limited experience. Transposing something immediate and self-evident – such as a useful object – to the realm of signs equates to moving it away. It corresponds to putting a conventional pseudo reality between the thing and the human being, in an intervention whose only function is to destroy the experience of anything concrete. The mediation of signs seeks to elude. In prostitution, the act indicates a nonexistent love. Just like in prostitution, the form of emptied theses is a sign of an abandoned realization. In prostitution, the sign appears as a mask. The sign, in architecture, masks its own prostitution. Fleeing from a bitter and dirty reality, it dresses architecture up in the sweet sway of calming mystification. What was once aggression is now surrender. The falsifying gesture suppresses a positive attitude.

The repetition in this text of the same cause – compensation and fugue from a reality that no one wants to confront head on – is not only the fault of the author. Processes of substitution are fertile in their detouring ways, despite a simple initial motivation. Indeed, the very multiplicity of the evasions is part of the defense mechanism: any observation of such a mechanism reveals its fragilities, but while one evasion is demystified, the others go undetected, surreptitiously upholding the mask.

Sérgio Ferro, born 1938, is an architect, painter, and professor living in São Paulo and Grignan, France. In 1968, he fled Brazil and lived in exile for 30 years.

Alvaro Puntoni, Angelo Bucci, João Oswaldo Vilela, Brazilian National Pavilion for Expo '92, Seville, Spain, 1992. Top: Paulo Mendes da Rocha, Museu Brasileiro de Escultura, São Paulo, Brazil, 1995. Photos: Nelson Kon. All photos courtesy the authors.

Frederico Costa
& Jaime Solares Carmona

Urban Trauma And the Box

Throughout the 20th century, urbanization in Brazil was seen as a way to overcome the backwardness associated with rural life or the precariousness of occupying a vast territory. These transformations intensified the distance between the urban milieu and the country's tropical national identity, resulting in a feeling of loss. The violence and injustices of this urbanization in Brazil, and in Latin America more broadly, had a traumatic effect in the second half of the century, especially on architects and urban planners.

The result of this process was widely perceived as a tragedy by our discipline, especially during the intense rural migrations in the 1970s, as it led to the congested, chaotic, and precarious images that still characterize the urban centers and peripheries of the country today. Instead of recognizing the complicity of modern architectural ideologies in this process, a new generation of Brazilian architects doubled down on modernist principles and reaffirmed them as denial, differentiation, and resistance to urbanization, culminating in the recovery of the pure forms of early modernism, notably, the perfect prism – the box. This box is characterized by four main features: a "transparent roof" made of skylights; blind walls on all of its facades; suspension over the ground, with part of the building's program buried underground; and the plastic integrity of the cube inspired by absolute abstract forms. From the '80s onward, "market realism" replaced Manfredo Tafuri's "ideology of the Plan," which characterized the previous decade's developmentalism, finding its symbolic form in both the condominium and the so-called politically engaged architecture. In both cases, we see the same isolated spatial realities, strictly ordered and inserted as fragments in a disconnected urban reality, requiring increasingly contradictory integration strategies and separation devices.

According to urbanist Teresa Caldera, condominiums could be considered fortified enclaves designed with modernist planning tools. They are antisocial forms that share a feeling of response to urban fear with the box. Through a process of critical action of purification, architecture reacts in a narcissistic way, formally differentiating the building – representing the form – from the surrounding context – the formless. Thus, the relationship of the modern box with the urban context becomes similar to that of the gated community. Revived as an archetype of contemporary architecture, the box represents both a resistance against urbanization and an appeal for order in didactic contrast to urban chaos.

Box Genesis

The Museu Brasileiro de Escultura (MuBE), designed by Paulo Mendes da Rocha in 1987, marks the changing relationship between architecture and the city. Without renouncing modern architecture's rationalist and functionalist expressiveness, Mendes da Rocha still reacted to postmodern criticism. The building disappears as an object because it is mostly underground; a prestressed concrete beam assumes its place as the building's index. Although critics acknowledged the phenomenological qualities of this – the inability to fully grasp the structure in favor of its fragmentary exploration, including a roof with widely spaced supports – they paid less attention to how the form became autonomous, related less to the program and more to its surroundings, even if in a contrasting manner.

The building doesn't adhere to contextualism. The city is viewed through a critical lens, with suspicion, interpreted as wilderness, to be tamed by architecture, framed by and aligned with the free span. Its unity challenges the inescapable urban chaos. This posture explains why the portico does not face the avenue, thereby reinforcing it as the primary access. Instead, the beam is aligned perpendicularly to the avenue, subjecting the city to the aspirations of the project envisioned as a grand plaza, which could never be realized due to the enclosure of the area necessary for the building's functioning.

In parallel with the museum's construction, another emblematic building began to be designed. The Brazilian National Pavilion for Expo '92, in Seville, won a national design competition, generating controversies that would shape contemporary architectural practice. It was designed by three young São Paulo (Paulista) architects: Angelo Bucci, Alvaro Puntoni, and José Oswaldo Vilela, students of Mendes da Rocha, who was on the competition jury. Considering the traditional success of Brazilian modern architecture in World's Fairs, this group yearned to overcome the country's years of recession and dictatorship and restore Brazil's cultural and symbolic ties with world architecture.

Their winning project, an elongated and suspended concrete box, surprised the critics, not for any innovative qualities, but for affirming traditional ones. The proposal thus resisted the foreign postmodernist assault, drawing inspiration from São Paulo's brutalism. But the Brazilian government did not build the pavilion due to economic constraints. The box returned to the architectural scene, detached from reality as it had never been before. Brutalist form reappeared as soft and minimalist. The project model reveals no intention of rusticity. Over the years, thanks to improved construction techniques and the recurrence of exposed concrete as a finishing option, brutality had been refined, roughness disappeared, and texture gained the thinness of an image.

The interior of the pavilion not only reinterpreted the same strategies that comprise the building where so many young architects had studied at the Faculty of Architecture and Urbanism (FAU) at the University of São Paulo (1968), designed by João Batista Vilanova Artigas and Carlos Cascaldi, it also brought together other iconic formal solutions from the repertoire of modernism. These include free-floating slabs in an interior void connected by ramps and a pavilion-like crown atop the pavilion itself. The internal space is never completely enclosed, as the floor slabs rest on the side walls with no other supports in sight. Unlike the FAU, the café on the pavilion's roof introduces a specific type of view outward, like a periscope that casts an interested yet distanced gaze.

These two projects, the museum and the unbuilt pavilion, underscore the birth of contemporary Brazilian architecture, reinforcing the box's condition of pure autonomy, not as a denial of urban fragmentation, but as an active contrast to it. The box is both critical in its isolation and expressive in its rationality, which will gradually turn criticism of the real city into accommodation. The mere release of architecture from "extrinsic constraints" gives way to a calculated exaltation of the dominant values of the modern tradition through form: namely, tectonic expressiveness, constructive metalanguage, the representation of space as infinite and abstract through the dissolution of boundaries, the appearance of revealing materials "as found," and the elementarism of form.

The 2006 exhibition "Coletivo: Arquitetura Paulista Contemporânea" (Collective: Paulista Contemporary Architecture) offered an overview of the new generation's work in the same year Mendes da Rocha won the Pritzker Prize. The exhibition was one of the main manifestations of the operative critique that gave shape and cohesion to this design practice, guided by common ideological and conceptual principles and evident formal affinities. The catalog's text, by Ana Luiza Nobre, Ana Vaz Milheiro, and Guilherme Wisnik, attested to a deliberately outdated novelty. Wisnik and a group of young architects from São Paulo had curated the Brazilian Pavilion at the 10th Venice Architecture Biennale in the same year, presenting São Paulo through their view of what Brazilian architecture should be.

The archetype of the box is supported by the notion of form, even though the architects continue to deny the intention of being guided by formal aspirations. This neomodernist revival relies on common design procedures, resulting in form's primacy (distracted or unconscious) and a more pronounced homogenization of formal solutions. The box, born as a form of critical autonomy, became mere social differentiation, betraying the aesthetic and ethical aspirations of the modernist avant-garde. The more this architecture produces levitating cubes, the more its affiliation with anti-urban isolationism becomes clear. If this "antiformalism" produces the same form over and over again, then it betrays its functionalist discourse, becoming hostage to the "image" of the box. Converted into images and inserted into the flow of symbolic exchanges, this architecture becomes what functionalist modernism tried to avoid from the beginning, namely formalism.

Therefore, form once again becomes a priority for analysis. When we speak of the box, we refer to legitimized architecture, ideologically oriented by a belief in rationality and its supposed moral virtues, which guide a vague idea of the social role of the architect but historically repeat that self-deception about its social possibilities. This syntactic vocabulary renewed itself as a reaction to postmodern pluralism, but in a social context different from its original formulations, making the box's production of images more closely related to postmodern aspirations. After all, in this contradictory position, the box can be seen as both innovative and traditionalist simultaneously.

Box Expansion

The failure to build the Expo '92 pavilion exemplifies the waning enthusiasm of the state to promote a national identity under emergent neoliberalism. Despite the globalization and liberalization process in the 1990s, Brazil was trying to create a postdictatorship social democracy. Until then, architects were part of a small but influential intellectual middle class that

MMBB, Escola FDE F1-Campinas, São Paulo, Brazil, 2003. Photo: Nelson Kon.

limited modern architecture's emancipatory ambitions to academic debates. The return to democracy fueled the hope of spreading this architecture to advance social transformation.

This culminated, in 2009, with the launch of the most extensive housing program in the country's history, Minha Casa, Minha Vida (MCMV), which became famous for building more than a million low-income houses nationwide. However, the main criticism of the program came from architects and urban planners who highlighted the perverse effects of urban disarticulation – that is, building of houses far from public services or transportation – that the program deepened. MCMV was implemented primarily as a financial operation, devoid of qualitative design criteria, thereby distancing architects and urban planners from relevant decisions throughout the program's implementation.

Before this new trauma of national urbanization, architects from São Paulo spread the box to express the egalitarian horizon of democracy. The Fundação para o Desenvolvimento da Educação (FDE) is the organization responsible for building schools in various cities in the State of São Paulo. Through it, in the early 2000s, several architecture firms designed small and medium-sized prefabricated schools. The architects who designed the FDE criteria for construction efficiency aimed to reduce construction costs and to restore modern form to its functionalist foundations. The limitation of materials and construction techniques favored a certain homogenization, and the formal purity and serialization of the buildings promoted a positive image of order in contrast to the precarious urbanization of the peripheries, where the schools were usually located. The facades communicate rationality, like a giant mute billboard. Still, the main facades, with greater visual eloquence, do not always correspond to the primary access. They result from a nonhierarchical organization of the building, without front or back,

From top: Terra e Tuma, Casa Vila Matilde, São Paulo, Brazil, 2015. Photo: Pedro Kok.
MMBB, Casa e Estúdio na Vila Romana, São Paulo, Brazil, 2006. Photo: Nelson Kon.
UNA Arquitetos, Casa Barreirinhas, São Paulo, Brazil, 2002. Photo: Nelson Kon.

Tacoa Arquitetos Associados, Adriana
Varejão Gallery, Minas Gerais, Brazil,
2008. Photo: Eduardo Eckenfels.

oriented on the site primarily by the layout of the structural
system and not by the program.

Shading elements, like metallic brise-soleils, are often used
to achieve formal integrity. Brise-soleils, reminiscent of the
traditional *cobogó*, which introduces shading and environmental comfort, are linked to a strategy of volumetric integrity –
filling gaps in the facade to form a perfect volume – and also
mediate between the public and the private, as is the case with
colonial-era lattices. In turn, the concrete block becomes a fundamental material for understanding the semantic reinterpretation of modernism in this sprawl. It temporarily resolves the
disjunction between the industrialization of construction and
modern architectural language. Although partly handcrafted,
the blocks appear to be an economically viable option in relation to reinforced concrete. Their modularity responds to the
desire to rationalize the construction, while their materiality –
apparent concrete – does not break with the brutalist aesthetic.

Casa Vila Matilde, designed by Terra e Tuma, illustrates
this point. Constructed from a custom-made metalwork
frame with concrete block, it demonstrates a clear desire to
differentiate from the surrounding clay brick houses. The
contrast between the "under-construction" appearance of
vernacular Brazilian favelas and the "industrial" look of
modern-inspired contemporary architecture reiterates the
oppositions of the urban as a reality. The critical success of
this award-winning house not only reflects the supposed
potential of this architectural solution but also testifies to
widespread and popular adherence to the taste of the intellectual elites, reconciling social inequalities through the symbolism of a supposedly radical aesthetic equality.

Rizoma Arquitetura, Lygia Pape
Gallery, Brumadinho – Minas
Gerais, Brazil, 2012. Top: Arquitetos
Associados, Miguel Rio Branco
Gallery, Brumadinho – Minas Gerais,
Brazil, 2010. Photos: Leonardo Finotti.

Private homes have also contributed to the dissemination of the box. In 2006, Casa e Estúdio na Vila Romana by MMBB recovered elements from the Corbusian canon. The project detaches the box from the ground, and, like MuBE, places the atelier underground. Although the project resonates with the multiplication of public land, neither the steep terrain, the perimeter wall, nor the context in which the work is located supports any argument for a prototype of urbanity, as was intended in Villa Savoye. On the other hand, Casa Barreirinhas, by UNA Arquitetos, built in 2002, replaces the concrete box's rusticity with a white volume, supported on stone walls but using the same strip window. In both cases, the presence of Corbusier's five points is blatantly obvious.

Distressed Box

It is not uncommon for the State of Minas Gerais, north of São Paulo, to stand out in contrast. In the small town of Brumadinho, the Inhotim Institute, created in 2004, has become the largest open-air museum in the world. In addition to the magnificent landscape, the park unites a variety of works of art and exhibition pavilions to form an art park amid the Atlantic Forest, not unlike a utopian model of a modernist city. However, instead of the chaotic urban sprawl of São Paulo, the idyllic fantasy of Minas Gerais stands out for its variation, pluralism, and formal freedom. That is, until the homogenizing force of the box invaded this lost paradise with the arrival, in 2008, of the Adriana Varejão Gallery, by Tacoa Arquitetos. The gallery is the pure expression of a floating concrete cube. It leans on a hill that is molded to receive it and cantilevers over a reflecting pool. This gallery has become a benchmark for subsequent galleries designed by local architects who continue to push this archetype to the limits of its formal integrity.

The Miguel Rio Branco Gallery, designed by Arquitetos Associados and completed in 2010, can be seen as a direct translation of the box in Minas Gerais. The architects embraced the box's contradictions and expressive and conceptual potential, abandoning its most dogmatic aspects to produce a volume covered with Corten steel plates that refer both to local mining activity and to Corten's recurring use in renowned foreign projects of the 2000s. However, the most striking feature, which marks a change in the box archetype, is the tension between the pure volume of the box and the break from the principle of elemental simplicity with a distorted and dynamic form. This tension is also present in the 2012 Lygia Pape Gallery, by Rizoma Arquitetura.

Isay Weinfeld, Santos Augusta Building, Cerqueira César, Brazil, 2017. Photo: Fernando Guerra. Right: Studio MK27, Paraty House, Paraty, Brazil, 2009. Photo: Nelson Kon.

The volumetric distortion here suggests an intention both to adhere to and differ from the box model as well as to update it. While exploring the expressive possibilities of the box form with more freedom, they remain faithful to its axioms: unity, volumetric austerity, a preference for abstraction over traditional or familiar architectural elements, and materiality "as found," among others. In this dreamlike environment, the box is liberated from the asceticism that gave rise to this archetype in the city and evolves with a touch of mannerism. Minas Gerais's difference regarding the Paulista's aesthetic militancy and the strong influence of its postmodern moment from the 1980s allows this subtle but essential differentiation from the box.

Box Smoothing
If in Minas Gerais the box is released from its simplicity through distortion, another group of architects in São Paulo explores the box in a minimalistic fashion. They reinterpret the box archetype not as a tectonic system but through its expressive potential as an abstract form. Often there is a softening of the box's surfaces, culminating in what we can call the "white box," an exteriorization of the classic "white cube." Visual cohesion takes precedence over revealing structural components and exposing materials. The projects create an aseptic harmony and a sophisticated scenic uniformity through moldings, ceilings, wood slats, translucent elements, and golden plates. Praise for detail replaces the praise for technique, the expression of noble materials, and refinement. The pioneering exponents of this trend are Isay Weinfeld and Studio MK27. Other notable firms include Felipe Hess

Andrade Morettin Arquitetos, Instituto Moreira Salles, São Paulo, Brazil, 2017. Photo: Nelson Kon.

Arquitetos, Bernardes Arquitetura, Jacobsen Arquitetura, Studio Arthur Casas, and Bloco Arquitetos. For this group, midcentury American houses and the work of Mexican architect Aurelio Martinez Flores in Brazil became more relevant than brutalist references.

The Paraty House, from 2009, by Studio MK27, synthesizes this typological evolution. It introduces two significant innovations. The first is the composition of two or more boxes to accommodate more extensive programs, especially on challenging terrain. The second is the framed face of the box, which is generally open or transparent and exposing the negativity of the interior void as a form of expression. This latter innovation reinforces the dissolution between interior and exterior, another modernist trope. The strategy of "stacking boxes" also favored the verticalization of this typology without losing cohesion, as seen in the the 360° Building, from 2013, and the Santos Augusta Building, from 2017, both by Isay Weinfeld.

Among the most significant projects in the metropolitan landscape, the 2011 competition for the new unit of the Instituto Moreira Salles in São Paulo presented an opportunity to explore the verticalization of large-scale cultural programs. The winning project, by Andrade Morettin Arquitetos, was built in 2017 and consolidated a particular characteristic of the firm, which frequently stood out for its exploration of new lightweight and translucent materials that replace the brutality of concrete. It was the only firm in the competition to explore the appeal of transparency as a symbolic element that connects the interior (institution) and exterior (public). Even so, the totality of the box remains, albeit translucent and divided by an intermediate slit that breaks its verticality.

Box Explosion

The strategy of avant-garde shock continued to be practiced by Bucci, who ultimately explored the formal collapse of the box archetype. However, this collapse did not necessarily represent a refusal but rather a kind of affirmative negation of its fundamental principles like formal tectonic purity and the indivisibility of space. His 2011 Casa de Fim de Semana and 2009 Casa em Ubatuba are examples of this formal explosion, which reorients the synthesis of the architectural form from the object (box) to the profusion of objects (box components). And even though the box can always be traced, the integral vision of the form disappears. It ceases to be the enclosure of space, as if an explosion abruptly removed the walls. Only the rooms remain, suspended in the air, like

organs in an invisible body. By denying the iconography of the box, each element becomes both a potential image and a denial of the reduction of architecture to a single image simultaneously – the unveiling of everything as a simulacra par excellence.

More recently, the same concept of fragmentation shaped a project in São Paulo by Arquitetos Associados. The Pina Contemporânea, a 2018 expansion of the São Paulo State Pinacoteca, under the direction of curator Jochen Volz, former artistic director of the Inhotim Institute, was the backlash that consecrated the architects from Minas Gerais in the Paulista tradition. The project was designed to virtually expand the historic building restored in 1998 by Mendes da Rocha, incorporating existing constructions like a modernist school and a pavilion in an eclectic style. But the so-called

urban axis that would connect the Pinacoteca do Estado to
the back of the Parque da Luz does not materialize due to
the service ramp, discontinuing any integration between the
back street and the park. The large central span is built at the
expense of the building's functionality. Just like MuBE, the
galleries become secondary spaces, making the deactivation
of the existing school and the enormous construction efforts
almost irrational. Even the restaurant, which acts as a periscope that mediates and distances the city from the building,
seems dislocated. Why not use this valuable space as a gallery,
putting the restaurant on the ground level and thus allowing
it to connect with the city? The ill-fated attempt to insert new
materials into the São Paulo repertoire, notably wood, makes
it clear that precarious detailing meets poor execution. The
sizeable transparent roof, a fundamental element of the box,
was overlaid on the entire complex like a napkin that unifies
all the shards of shattered glass. The result is halfway between
fragment and whole, in which the syntax of the box is maintained even if its components are separated.

After all, Mendes da Rocha's architecture consolidated itself
as a fundamental reference for this contemporary Brazilian
syntax. International recognition, like the Praemium Imperiale
in Japan and the Golden Lion at the Venice Architecture
Biennale, both awarded in 2016, strengthened his totemic position for the younger generations that both work with and

worship him, but also cast a long shadow that has made it difficult for new initiatives to flourish. We can also see this modern revival in the constant updates of the International Style in foreign contexts, for which this production is also a reference. However, beyond the traumas of urbanization, the reality of Brazilian territory and its cities produced their own discourses and spatial practices, with or without the participation of architects, increasingly highlighting issues beyond the narrow point of view of architectural tradition. Gradually, it has become evident that Brazil does not fit in the box.

Unboxing

How can we have an overview of architecture beyond the box? Why does it seem so difficult to envision architecture without this self-referential view of modernist production?

The genealogy of the box is not the only development in the modernist and brutalist production of the heroic architecture between 1930 and 1960 in Brazil. The work of Lina Bo Bardi is an example of how to reinterpret this modern heritage. Her most prominent work, the SESC Pompéia, from 1986, was one of the most significant achievements in 20th-century Brazilian architecture. Bo Bardi's project pointed a way out of the urban impasse that drove the next generation to the dilemma of the box. The history of the original factory functions in the project as an urban reminiscence, while new prismatic volumes reconstruct positive and negative spaces that differ from the abstract and generic "free space" of modernist voids. Despite providing seeming isolation, the complex maintains continuity with the surrounding urban areas, preserving the scale of these urban situations and engaging with the typical verticality of São Paulo's urban landscape.

The architects who formed Brasil Arquitetura worked with Bo Bardi on her final projects and attempted to continue her legacy. However, in 2012, one of their principal works, Praça das Artes, failed to replicate the vibrant atmosphere of the street in SESC Pompéia. Their internal streets are merely widened alleys surrounded by "back facades," blind walls of tinted concrete that, despite aspiring to Bo Bardi's artisanal expressiveness, result in nothing more than an antisocial texture. Despite the much richer urban situation in the heart of downtown, the Praça das Artes retreats from any meaningful dialogue with the real city. Instead, it becomes a series of spectral masses that echo the scales and rhythms of the surrounding buildings, not as analogy but as a disillusioned continuity, a faded memory incapable of generating urbanity

Lina Bo Bardi, SESC Pompéia, São Paulo, Brazil, 1986. Photo: Nelson Kon. Right: Brasil Arquitetura, Praça das Artes, São Paulo, Brazil, 2012. Photo: Nelson Kon.

itself. The irregular windows look at the city as if they cannot form their own viewpoint, and the inner street, more like a highway, fails to connect with the surrounding streets due to a gate that opens and closes depending on institutional whims. Even if the connection were unobstructed, as the architects desired, why would anyone choose an arid, castle-like alleyway when they could walk on the adjacent well-lit street lined with tiny jewels of Paulista eclecticism?

The youngest generation of architects in São Paulo seems to radicalize the box or detach from it, but the box is never totally overcome. Among the most exciting cases are two offices in São Paulo that polarize a more orthodox connection and a more experimental independence from this lineage: 23 SUL Arquitetura and Vão. Projects by 23 SUL are devout syntheses of their predecessors' work, many of whom are colleagues and former professors. The box's formal integrity is evident in projects like their 2014 Batistini Bus Terminal and other transport terminals, even in new situations and with new materials. These architects refuse the idea of functionalism as outdated or inappropriate and use tectonic expressionism as an alibi against accusations of traditional modernism. The supposed universality of technique – as a representation of radical equality and neutral taste – also opposes the notion of regional identity and the artistic tradition of São Paulo. Less evident is the arbitrariness with which São Paulo has historically transformed its local particularities into notions of neutrality and universality through its economic dominance over the nation.

Sometimes this paradox leads to unpleasant contradictions, as in 23 SUL's 2018 Morumbi Station. The primary cohesive element of the station is the roof – a metal grid

infilled with glass panels. It not only reinforces the grid as a metaphor for rationality but also unifies a program that is difficult for the architects to control. Developed using German roofing technologies, the architects aimed to make this "magic carpet" as thin as possible in order to span the enormous gaps required by the complex program. However, this technological sophistication did not adequately address the demand for protection from rains typical of the local climate, which has since become a problem, with constant leaks and internal pooling.

Vão remains interested in the modernist repertoire but their references are pluralistic. Their interface with contemporary art, such as their exhibition design for the 35th Bienal de São Paulo, in 2023, enriches their work by drawing on sources beyond architecture, fostering a broad approach to architecture that demonstrates a willingness to revive a certain avant-garde appeal.

The Bienal happens in Pavilhão Ciccillo Matarazzo, designed by Oscar Niemeyer in 1957, which can be described as a large rectangular pavilion with a ramp that connects all of its slabs through a central void. By constructing half-height white partitions like the building's walls, Vão negates the Niemeyer void. This seemingly rebellious gesture aims to neutralize the inescapable presence of the building over the works of art. The architects use elements of the building to make it a captive of its own architecture. On the upper floor, the void is enclosed in a continuous organic form that frees the rest of the floor. In contrast, on the level below, the void is consumed by the negative space designed as a result of the mass built on the pavilion's perimeter. By rejecting the void, which gives identity to the pavilion, the office makes a progressive and regressive manifesto, simultaneously reinforcing the "white cube" strategy on one floor while freeing the space on another.

Vão's architectural repertoire diversifies and embraces less orthodox and hegemonic aspects of contemporary, modernist, and vernacular traditions. This breadth results in projects ranging from pure descendants of the modern houses of the 1960s, such as their Casa Joanópolis, of 2023, to timeless experiments that evoke Scandinavian empiricism, like the 2022 Casa São João da Boa Vista, or contemporary encounters with vernacular tradition, as seen in the 2020 Casa São José do Barreiro.

The widely publicized works of these two offices still reveal the recurrence of modernist tradition as a form of contemporary legitimation. Institutional and critical initiatives seeking other alternatives in the face of this legitimization are still relatively recent and rare.

Large Brazilian cities impose themselves on architects as inevitable material realities. They are neither the result of a rational, colonial, and homogeneous planning process nor completely disconnected fragments in the territory. In this way, architecture plays an increasingly central role in using, understanding, and representing these complex realities. As the logic of the condominium establishes itself at the center of the country's public realm, the desire for order seeks a single and clear answer. The condominiums accomplish what the box only simulated, thus portraying the most regressive side of this architectural dogma. On the other hand, as we start to criticize the box and to explore other architectural possibilities, we can overcome the trauma of urbanization and face the challenges it created head-on.

Frederico Costa is an architect, professor and PhD student at UNICAMP in the history and theory of architecture and urbanism. Jaime Solares Carmona is a PhD student at Yale University.

Felipe Mesa
& Federico Mesa

Re-activism

The following statements represent what we believe architecture is, defined after its construction and not a priori. This architecture "reacts" positively to its context, engaging with the political possibilities it enacts, thus defining an "activist" dimension to our practice. Re-activism is therefore a rear-guard position, a type of utopia of the immediate present. We understand the now as the mediation between the past – learning from almost 25 years of professional and academic practice – and the future: architecture understood as immediate reality. We do not propose a dogma but a flexible view that is under construction. It is organized around three major principles that define our praxis: permeability, positive prospective realism, and partial pacts.

Permeability

The architectural project is a permeable, bioclimatic, and sustainable phenomenon at several scales: environmental, urban, material, and social. We do not design hermetic boxes isolated from the socioenvironmental context.

Permeability: PLAN: B Arquitectos with JPRCR Arquitectos, Orquideorama, Medellín, Colombia, 2006. All photos Alejandro Arango. Courtesy the authors.

The architectural project is a complementary geometry, flexible and adaptable to the context and the environment. Buildings must be available configurations. We do not work with closed forms or programs.

Permeability: PLAN: B Arquitectos, Hontanares School, El Retiro, Colombia, 2012.

The architectural project requires a reversed design process that moves from the forces of the context – cultural, environmental, and economic – toward our inclinations, allowing for encounters with unexpected phenomena. We do not work from our inclinations but toward them.

Permeability: PLAN: B Arquitectos, House in El Alto, Envigado, Colombia, 2014.

Prospective Realism

The architectural project is a convergent phenomenon and a hybrid configuration that incorporates various technologies, materials, and socioenvironmental realities. It condenses the recurring contradictions of our ecological, social, and economic realities. It is not pure, abstract, clean, or minimalist. We do not avoid mixing and contact. We are not afraid to get dirty.

Prospective Realism: PLAN: B Arquitectos, Amaluna House, Envigado, Colombia, 2022.

A built building is more radical than its representation can be. We do not work to produce drawings but to construct interactions between material and affective phenomena. We prefer to generate a conversation in which any detail is critical rather than to reduce phenomena to their main forces or poetic figures. We embrace the difficulties of life and construction.

Prospective Realism: PLAN: B Arquitectos, Santo Domingo Savio Kindergarten, Medellín, Colombia, 2011.

The architectural project is an incomplete configuration that is activated by daily life and that welcomes and supports it. Tectonic and affective phenomena are complementary and simultaneous. Form for form's sake is overrated.

Prospective Realism: PLAN: B Arquitectos with Giancarlo Mazzanti, Four Sport Facilities, Medellín, Colombia, 2010.

107

Provisional Agreements

The architectural project expresses a provisional agreement and admits various materials, geometries, technologies, and strategies to emerge from this negotiation. It is a changing and inclusive agreement that manifests and absorbs the diverse constraints involved in the design process. We consider restrictions the basis of the creative phenomenon. We don't need creative freedom but creative commitment.

Provisional Agreements: PLAN: B Arquitectos, San Vicente Community Center, Antioquia, Colombia, 2016.

The architectural project is imperfect. It requires improvements and adaptations over time. It should be resilient, but it needs maintenance and care. We are not obsessed with efficiency and perfection. We understand defects as singular qualities that give the work character and personality.

Provisional Agreements: PLAN: B Arquitectos, Siete Vueltas School, Antioquia, Colombia, 2016.

The architectural project works better as a naked body exhibiting various systems. It is often enough to articulate some bones, arteries, and muscles. We don't focus on costumes. We like the idea of naked architecture without veils.

Provisional Agreements: PLAN: B Arquitectos, House in La Siria, Antioquia, Colombia, 2022.

The architectural project expands our individual and social phenotype. Architecture is natural and part of the body. We do not work by building differences between the natural and artificial worlds; for us, they are the same: houses, anthills, honeycombs, shelters, and nests.

Provisional Agreements: PLAN: B Arquitectos, House in Ríocedro, Córdoba, Colombia, 2011.

Felipe Mesa and Federico Mesa are brothers and the founding directors of PLAN: B Arquitectos, a studio in Medellín, Colombia.

The urban conditions of São Paulo, Brazil, (left) are mirrored by similar conditions in Medellín, Colombia. All photos by the author.

Mariana Wilderom

Monumentalizing The Everyday

I write from São Paulo, an untamed city that constantly and violently reshapes itself. Perceived as an incomplete rosary of disconnected cities, as the poet activist Mário de Andrade would say, this palimpsest city now prides itself on having evolved from building one house per hour in the early 20th century to erecting two buildings per day in the 21st century. What crumbles under this neighborhood-erasing real estate frenzy is not only the affective memory of everyday urban life in São Paulo but also the hope of confronting this vast phenomenon of *deterritorialization* through a critical design stance or any disciplinary tools in architecture and urbanism.

The disfigurement of space-time relations in São Paulo, fueled by an international real estate market, ultimately radicalizes its generative process. The city itself arises from the production of non-places. Since agro-export capital laid the tracks for industrialization, the urban fabric has lacked cohesion, fragmenting into lot-by-lot partitioning and sidelining the social base from rightful participation in urban processes. In this city, shaped mostly by an explosive, segregating, and exclusionary process, some people live in the interstices, while others survive on the peripheries.

The inability to create an urban landscape that embodies collectivity and social justice is part of the Capitalocene's environmental tragedy. Here, urbanization has subjugated the idealized tropical nature, alternately treating it as a resource or an obstacle. From this historical perspective, our disciplinary trajectory appears to have faltered. Faced with the escalating challenges of producing urbanization without producing a city, architecture, in its hegemonic framework, has opted for anti-urban, aesthetic schemes. These schemes, despite their intent for social transformation, have not addressed real urban space. Urbanism, seen more as planning than urban design, has been left to navigate the political struggle for the right to the city.

Thus the analytical framework presented here sharpens a critique of strategies that favor the "self-sufficient singularity of the unit" over the "universalizing extroversion of the module" typical of European modernization.[1] This subjuga-

1. Luiz Recamán, "As virtualidades do morar: o espaço impossível da casa," in *Artigas e a metrópole*, eds. Luiz Recamán and Leandro Medrano (São Paulo: FAUUSP, 2015), 55.

111

tion to objectual architecture feels like a mirage, an expectation – that this architectural conception would become the rule rather than the exception in the urban landscape – continuously revealed to be an illusion. The derivations of this fragmented aesthetic scheme, imposed as exemplary – and visible in the works of masters Oscar Niemeyer and João Batista Vilanova Artigas – persist today in an even more fragmented and abstract ethical-technical way through routinized design strategies. These include the aesthetic and discursive exploration of minimalist structural solutions in reinforced concrete, as well as variations in characteristic constructive details such as fenestration, metalwork, ramps, zenithal lighting, and other spatial effects, echoing the way Paulo Mendes da Rocha articulated this lexicon.

Balancing conciseness and precision, these strategies reinforce the expectation of the hermetic, microcosmic object: a self-centered unit. By distancing itself from the context – without alluding to, modifying, or nullifying it – this approach creates a space-time suspended from reality, awaiting the moment when society transforms to such an extent that the walls protecting these objects will fall and the city will become a continuum of juxtaposed architectural jewels.[2]

By focusing on the nexus between building and city, what Lefebvre calls the "micro-urbanistic" and "macro-architectural,"[3] criticism can turn limits into thresholds. It is at this level that an essential mediation occurs between urban society and its emancipatory potential, even if it is residual.

Mirror

To see Medellín, Colombia, one must first dispel the stereotypical images of this city, once the most violent in the world and now celebrated for its turnaround. The recent narratives often highlight the revolution in mobility infrastructure, the creation of public facilities, and urban projects reaching the deprived and violent peripheries, usually oversimplifying the process. In examining the historical and contemporary conditions, institutional programs, financing methods, legal frameworks, and urban planning tools, I navigated an intergenerational network of collaborating architects, marked by diverse and intertwined authors. What captivates me is how the discipline operates at the interfaces of these conditions, suggesting the nuances of its agency. Architecture and urbanism play a strategic part in this social transformation, not just serving as emblems, but also reclaiming the public sphere lost during the turbulent 1990s.

2. Mariana Wilderom and Luiz Recamán, "The Meaning of Counter-Hegemony Possibilities in Architecture," *VIRUS* 24, trans. Isabel de Carvalho Ferreira (August 2022), https://vnomads.eastus.cloudapp.azure.com/ojs/index.php/virus/article/download/734/1042/1851.
3. See Henri Lefebvre, *Tiempos equívocos* (Madrid: Kairos, 1967).

Boldarini Arquitetos, Cantinho do Céu, São Paulo, 2007. The project recovers a reservoir area, weaving it into the socio-spatial fabric.

Medellín mirrors São Paulo's fate, with nature domesticated by an agro-export–driven economy financing late industrialization. Medellín prides itself on being a supraregional economic engine yet can appear equally arid and highway-centric, with urban forms of segregation perpetuating differentiated access to citizenship. However, Medellín's valley topography, eternal spring, and scenic sky not only captivate the senses, they also contribute to making the metropolis tangible. The valley's configuration and its 2.5 million inhabitants maintain a sense of collectivity mediated by nature, in contrast with São Paulo's sprawling urban area with over 12 million inhabitants.

The difference between Brazilian and Colombian modern traditions is evident in the latter's shift away from Corbusian influences to seek references with distinct construction technologies. While brick, a traditional small and versatile construction unit, characterizes Colombian production, concrete dominates Brazilian architecture, imposing totalizing forms and intentions. Repetitive and adaptable, brick accommodates any form, function, and circumstance. Concrete, with its large-scale structural forms and assertiveness, demands hermetic gestures. This distinction is possibly the foundational divergence in the relationship between "text and context" in the architecture of these two cities.

Strategic Urban Interventions Department, Articulated Life Units (UVA) la Libertad, Medellín, 2015. The city initiative created parks around water tanks in high, peripheral poor neighborhoods.

Integrated Urban Projects (PUI), Metrocable system and a station plaza in a recomposed urban fabric, Medellín. Top and middle: Latitud Taller de Arquitectura y Ciudad, Parques del Río, Medellín, 2016. The park prioritizes public space over urban roadways along the riverfront.

Kaleidoscope

A kaleidoscopic approach to the analysis of architectural projects in São Paulo and Medellín delves into a critical inventory. This process stabilizes some common disciplinary issues, formulated as categories, by bringing spatial paradigms closer to their potential. Although provisional, these thematic categories function as analytical frameworks. They aim to highlight recurring issues within the discipline and critically examine the ways in which architecture responds to the complexities of real urban contexts, shaping what can be termed "architectural reactions." These design formulations do not present fully defined aesthetic, functional, and social objectives, but they find points of contact between social processes and the discipline of architecture and urbanism that push these architectures to develop a projective language to react to the status quo through daily practice.

Infrastructure and Landscape Reconfiguration

In a kaleidoscopic comparison of projects in these cities, urban infrastructure is approached not only for its function but also as leverage for reconfiguring the deteriorated urban landscape (both social and environmental) and to claim a new one that amplifies and collectivizes symbolic values. The 2007 Cantinho do Céu in São Paulo, by Boldarini Arquitetos,[4] addresses the urban recovery of the Billings reservoir area. The reservoir is an important water source for São Paulo. Since pollution poses a significant public health risk, the architects responded by shifting from a purely technical approach to one that emphasizes social and urban dimensions. They avoided unnecessary demolition and remained committed to creating a readable urban fabric by highlighting the previously hidden body of water and offering residents a unique landscape. Different ground qualities, including elevated pathways crossing the riparian vegetation and paved trails, were woven into the interstices of a surgical removal of precarious housing to create public space and build spatial continuities and coherences. Notably, there is no totalizing architectural object. What stands out is the immense body of water revealed by this subtle yet expansive aesthetic strategy, which wielded a profound transformative power over the socio-spatial fabric, reverberating through the community.

These design procedures – qualifying through subtraction, connection, and cohesion, and closely aligned with reality – can also be observed in the Unidades de Vida Articulada, or Articulated Life Units, by the Strategic Urban

4. A more detailed analysis of this project is my "Reclaimed urban landscapes. Architectural reactions that reframe infrastructure," *Dearq* 33 (May 2022): 54–65, https://doi.org/10.18389/dearq33.2022.06.

Interventions Department (DIUS) in the Public Enterprises of Medellín. In this case, removing the walls around the city's water supply tanks, which are located in the high, peripheral poor neighborhoods, revealed a network of new public spaces. Architecture had the task of integrating these technical and infrastructural enclaves into their communities through new pathways and stairs. These projects now provide panoramic views of the city. Small buildings representing the core programmatic elements of the UVAs support this spatial scheme, expanding it with their roofs and providing community rooms for classes and meetings, etc.

The 2016 Parques del Río project in Medellín, by Latitud Taller de Arquitectura y Ciudad, revitalized the Medellín River axis. Presented as an exemplary urban model, it has the potential for replication throughout the valley, prioritizing the production of public space over roadways, advocating for better environmental and urban conditions, and increasing the presence of green areas for public enjoyment. A segment of this park has been implemented in the city's center, showcasing the potential of the project's totalizing vision. Although constructing and burying the road arteries along the river was controversial, raising protests against the disruptions in the already chaotic daily traffic, public contestation gave way to an intense, exultant, and festive collective appropriation of the newly created public realm. This space now pulses in different ways every day.

The metamorphosis of infrastructure landscapes is also visible in the metrocable system. In addition to reducing the daily commutes of periphery residents from hours to minutes, it created multi-level stations with numerous plazas, overcoming their role as mere technical apparatuses. Through the Integrated Urban Projects (PUI), the urban fabric surrounding the metrocable stations was also recomposed. The stations repeat the effect of viewpoints, woven into the visual web from the periphery to the center and vice versa.

Disjunction and Opening of the Form-Function Relationship

The transcendence of the formal-programmatic functionalist relationship – without succumbing to disciplinary abstraction or autonomy – is analyzed here through the gaps or overlaps that some projects, based on traditional programs such as schools, cultural centers, libraries, and parks, seem to propose. This movement aligns with the spatial and programmatic ideal of a social condenser influenced by real-world

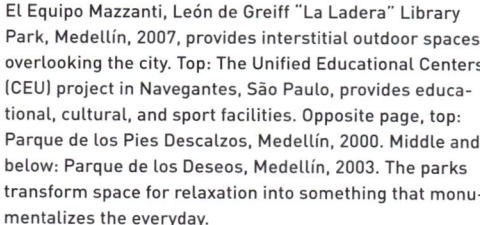

El Equipo Mazzanti, León de Greiff "La Ladera" Library Park, Medellín, 2007, provides interstitial outdoor spaces overlooking the city. Top: The Unified Educational Centers (CEU) project in Navegantes, São Paulo, provides educational, cultural, and sport facilities. Opposite page, top: Parque de los Pies Descalzos, Medellín, 2000. Middle and below: Parque de los Deseos, Medellín, 2003. The parks transform space for relaxation into something that monumentalizes the everyday.

Parque de los Pies Descalzos, Medellín, 2000.

contingencies. Bringing social services closer to the spontaneous practices of daily life creates new kinds of urban public space and challenges the historical relationship between social services and citizenship. They integrate state programs but seem to resist becoming components of an incomplete and regulated citizenship, thereby avoiding the reduction of the citizen to a mere user or consumer.

The CEU (Unified Educational Centers) typology, with around 50 units currently in operation, was implemented by the São Paulo municipal government over the past 20 years. These large complexes, which combine educational, cultural, and sports facilities, have made undeniable social contributions, but they also reveal certain limitations in their spatial paradigm. Built as enclosed architectural ensembles in vulnerable peripheral areas, they often limit spontaneous appropriation due to restricted access and surveillance. Their rigid relationship between form and function, as well as their scale and adherence to the objectual architectural tradition, has posed challenges to their integration with the urban context and local socio-spatial practices. In Medellín's projects, we seek alternative approaches that offer perspectives for addressing such complexities.

In Medellín, the programmatic domain of a library expands through formal extroversion, which spreads across different buildings in a park. In the 2007 León de Greiff "La Ladera" Library Park, by El Equipo Mazzanti, the tripartite elements of the freely accessible library-cum-park create interstitial spaces as important as the buildings themselves. In addition, the roof terraces serve as transition points for users to navigate the uneven terrain, forming small amphitheater-like areas with views of the city.

At Colegio Antonio Derka, by ObraNegra Arquitectos, the school roof is a large plaza that extends from the sidewalk and functions both as a colossal lookout and a simple building cover. It provides a public space, despite the topographical challenges and social vulnerability of the region, and also serves as a unique mediation device – a lookout boundary whose programmatic-formal elevation and monumental appeal protect students inside the building without relying on fences. More importantly, the project doesn't impose an idealized, impossible relationship between the community and the school's spaces. These buildings offer quality public services with the potential to transform not only access to a more dignified future through education and culture but also the very perception of the possibilities opened up by it. They promote adherence to a dignified urban imaginary and its experience in everyday life.

The Jardin Infantil Carpinelo by Ctrl G, an early childhood education center, uses cellular arrangements to expand urban relationships. Here, classrooms expand into internal gardens, opening up the pedagogical experience to a playful environment. At the same time, the building's perimeter softens the harsh conditions of surrounding poverty by turning interstitial spaces into small urban resting areas that allow things such as railings to be used as clotheslines. This strategy incorporates and elevates the real urban environment into a possible urbanity, ranging from private activities to collective public activities.

Monumentality and Everyday Life Beyond the Spectacular
When seen through the kaleidoscope, various projects suggest a monumentality with everyday practices. What is monumentalized varies and shifts from subject to strategy: roofs (Orquideorama), sidewalks (Antonio Derka), ground (Parque de los Deseos and Parque de los Pies Descalzos), infrastructure (UVAs, Cantinho do Céu, Metrocable, Parques del Rio), (Parque Biblioteca "La Ladera") and transitive relationships between domesticity, materiality, and landscape (Jardin Infantil Carpinelo, Parque Prado). The radicalization of aesthetic power in these projects reminds us of the distinctive force of the Brazilian modern tradition, which has gained worldwide recognition. Additionally, the spatial and symbolic tendencies of expansion and extroversion suggest a desire to anticipate or create the conditions for a collective engagement – a specific contribution from the Colombian examples. This engagement distances itself from a hasty association with the spectacular or self-centered objectuality. Its imagistic dimension does not intend to ignore or overshadow reality. In fact, it even partially radicalizes some aspects of reality.

This formulation of the monumentality of the everyday still requires further investigation, considering the historical significations of the monument. This new "new monumentality" – recalling the words of Leger, Giedion, and Sert in 1943[5] – elevates participation in the social and urban process. And it does not seem to succumb to urbanization without the city. By evoking an expanded collectivity and claiming the discipline's participation in it, this new monumentality avoids relegating the demand for revolutionary change to an atomized society.

5. See J. L. Sert, F. Leger, S. Giedion, "Nine Points on Monumentality," in Joan Ockman, ed., *Architecture Culture 1943–1968* (New York: Columbia Books of Architecture/Rizzoli, 1993).

Above and opposite page: Edgar Mazo, Parque Prado, Medellín, 2021. The design, which was a 2022 Mies Crown Hall Americas Prize finalist, interprets sustainable construction policies by integrating abandoned structures with new plantings and native vegetation.

Horizons

Through and against hierarchization, could there not be, here and there, architecturally or urbanistically, "something" that results from the existing mode of production, that is born from its contradictions, revealing them instead of covering them with a veil?
— Henri Lefebvre, 1985[6]

The analytical conjectures offered here ultimately defend criticism and its necessary radicality. I trust in its capacity to unveil limits and point out thresholds of transposition, embracing what Tafuri describes as a form of "critical destruction" when quoting Benjamin: "The destructive character sees nothing permanent. But for this very reason he sees ways everywhere."[7] This political-pedagogical demand allows disciplinary operations to resist the determining power structures that organize space and knowledge. In *Toward an Architecture of Enjoyment*, Lefebvre recognizes that the "mode of production" as a definitive system, taken to the extreme, means the annihilation of thought and action. Facing this issue is a task for humanity and its capacity to produce its own future, actively engaging in the transformation of reality, especially in light of the environmental emergency. Therefore, it remains vital to seek a critical framework capable of accessing the socio-spatial and environmental contents of our reality, to transform, through architecture and urbanism, the status quo, or at least to resist the destructive social logics of the contemporary world.[8]

Monumentalizing the everyday, distinct from the symbolism of modern abstraction, signals that a tabula rasa is no

6. Henri Lefebvre, "Prefácio: A Produção do Espaço" *Estudos Avançados* 27, no. 79 (2013): 123–132. (our translation)
7. Manfredo Tafuri, "Conversación con Manfredo Tafuri" *Materiales* (March 1983). Reprinted in *Tafuri en Argentina*, ed. Adrián Gorelik and Francisco Díaz (Santiago: Ediciones ARQ, 2019), 41.
8. Wilderom and Recamán.

longer viable. While all architectural projects operate within the constraints of capitalist logic, this approach sketches a critical reaction to the radicalization of abstract fragmentation imposed by this system. It seeks to reconfigure symbolic and spatial frameworks by working within and against the system's inherent contradictions. This approach conveys desolation while appealing to the symbolic desire of the monument. These aesthetic elevations transform everyday elements into something monumental, emerging from the emancipatory residue that still pulses in everyday practices. Grounded in the real but looking toward the future, this vision represents a last attempt at a concrete utopia. While this strategy depends on extra-architectural forces to be fully realized, it at least indicates a starting point for the reterritorialization of architecture.

Mariana Wilderom is a professor at Universidade São Judas Tadeu and postdoctoral fellow at Faculdade de Arquitetura e Urbanismo e de Design da Universidade de São Paulo. She contributed to the books *Marcenaria Baraúna: Móvel como Arquitetura* (2017), *Social Urbanism in Latin America* (2020), and *Architecture as Built Criticism* (2024).

José Luis Uribe Ortiz

From the Margins

Above and opposite page: Matias Zegers, Casa Hare Unahi Ika, Rapa Nui, Chile, 2020. Photos courtesy the architect.

In South America, which is characterized by both economic poverty and an abundance of natural resources, some of the most interesting contemporary architectural practices of recent decades have emerged. This economic-material dichotomy has nurtured a project logic based on the relationships that architects in the Southern Cone have established with local artisans, thereby shaping a unique architecture that is based on "place" and that draws on local customs for how each project might be built. These new South American architectural practices have developed work that is of global interest based on the rich and diverse local cultures they embody, all while accentuating the typological, material, technical, and spatial values associated with prosaic architecture, which forms the inhabitants' cultural imagination.

The South American territory is a living context that constantly agitates, motivates, and promotes these architectural practices. In the last few decades, various ways of making architecture have emerged, allowing us to say that there is no particular way of making architecture in South America. Some of these architectural practices have escaped the echoes of the International Style and instead promote openness during the design and construction process by recognizing local variables such as geographical, material, landscape, technical, and human dimensions, decanted in individual works that distance themselves from any authorial formalism. These practices have attracted international awards and recognition, such as the Mies Crown Hall Americas Prize awarded to Natura Futura in 2024 and Barclay & Crousse in 2018; the Golden Lion for Best Participant in the 2016 Venice Architecture Biennale awarded to Gabinete de Arquitectura; and the AR Emerging Architecture award given to Carla Juaçaba in 2018. The prizes acknowledge this work for mastering the multiscalar dimension of architecture and achieving a level of control that flows from the territory into the detail. These practices have also been internationally recognized for excellence and creativity that reflect a deep connection to South American material culture, incorporating traditional techniques in their construction processes.

Above and opposite page: Nicolás Campodonico, Capilla San Bernardo, La Playosa, Argentina, 2015. Photos courtesy the architect.

1. Iñaki Abalos, *Textos críticos* (Madrid: Ediciones Asimétricas, 2017), 52–53. My translation.
2. Juhani Pallasmaa, *Una arquitectura de la humildad* (Barcelona: Fundación Caja de Arquitectos, 2010), 135.

The language of contemporary architecture can be characterized as bringing together context-specific materials, without ornament, in a raw and sincere way, manifesting the honesty of earth, brick, stone, and wood. Considering material culture as a background that allows us to understand a society, architect Iñaki Ábalos, in his article "El que escucha la materia" (He who listens to material), refers to the creative processes of sculptor Eduardo Chillida. Ábalos writes: "In a language closer to Heidegger, [Chillida] spoke of listening to material, that his job consisted of letting it emerge – steel, wood, concrete, stone – materials all endowed with a temporal thickness, with an existential, ontological meaning, which the artist revealed."[1]

For Ábalos, material is a variable in a creative process mediated by the body, which interacts with it to reveal the physical properties that affect a construction. These properties have a greater meaning than simply material as mass and focus on a series of values that transcend the work, all guided by the hand of the craftsman.

The use of material is part of an approach that expresses the architectural object and gives new life to that material. Through the development of manual skills and techniques, materiality establishes links with local inhabitants via their imagination. A *material imagination*,[2] in Juhani Pallasmaa's words, focusing on recognition of the artisan, is a project

variable that allows us to understand a specific local culture. In that sense, the experiences surrounding construction processes associated with new architectural practices in South America could be considered small laboratories of material experimentation based upon the technical expertise of local artisans. The architect incorporates the artisan's knowledge of local materials during the planning stage, then actively participates in the construction of the architectural work, contributing to the craft with his own hands. Sometimes, this construction process is more interesting than the finished work

Claude Leví-Strauss, in his book *Wild Thought,* defines two cultural methods that establish the creation of objects and works. First is the engineer or scientist who uses reason and works based on concepts and structures to create mechanical systems that feature coherence, accuracy, and interchangeable parts. Then there is the bricoleur who, like a "savage," takes advantage of local materials and objects. These objects are recycled and reassembled, and new objects are manufactured and made of found parts. The latter constructive logic is associated with trust in the architect's ability to harness whatever materials the local environment provides and to coordinate those materials using the skills of local artisanal craftsmen.

A group of South American architectural practices that operate from the periphery has contributed to a disciplinary paradigm shift without falling into cryptic discourses, thus

Above and opposite page: Carla Juaçaba, Casa Rio Bonito, Nova Friburgo, Brazil, 2015. Photos: Nelson Kon. Courtesy the architect.

giving birth to a working method rooted in the honesty of the builder and of the materials.

In Chile, Matías Zegers uses a design repertoire based on opposing orders, such as the tectonics of structure, the weight associated with stereotomy, experimentation around material honesty, and the rootedness of experience concentrated in various trades of his rural context. Zegers has distanced himself from the style that typifies the new generation of Chilean architects by producing fresh work characterized by its defects in wall surfaces and the roughness of haptic experiences for the inhabitants. In a 2022 conversation Zegers said: *For me, architecture is about the interaction of people with what we build. This interaction is first of all physical, then philosophical. We perceive it with our senses, and our brain interprets it. We wanted to achieve a wall with the plastic expression of rammed earth but made of exposed concrete. We did many tests until we found the precise mixture of cement, pigments, aggregates. But what was interesting was that the whole team, from the client to the workers, shared the same idea of beauty. We were moved by the same things — the wall's imperfections, the changes of tone, a pebble that looked out, a shadow that lengthened with the sun shining on it, the story that appeared when a wall was uncovered.*[3]

The spaces Zegers conceived are seasoned with a nostalgia, reflecting his prioritization of experience over mere structural prowess or formal pomposity. This commitment to timelessness and to emotional connection with the environment reflects the architect's ethical and aesthetic position, transcending fashions and passing trends.

Along this line, Nicolás Campodonico, an architect who also curates, writes, and teaches in Rosario, Argentina, picks up the baton of the Rosario school of thought, established in the work of Jorge Scrimaglio, Rafael Iglesia, Gerardo Caballero, and Marcelo Villafañe. One of Campononico's most significant works is Capilla San Bernardo, which concentrates on the climatological passage of time articulated in the patina of its brick surface. In the chapel, it is possible to find a sum of global and local architectural references. It corresponds to a lost rural infrastructure of bodies, hermetic, heavy, and rough, that impose themselves as a middle point to connect the chromatic contrast of the green ground and blue sky – mono-material body, a still mass recognized by its contrast with nature.

In Brazil, where contemporary production is marked by a hegemony of modernist architecture, Carla Juaçaba provides a new and authentic approach. Far from the modernist

3. Excerpt of the conversation between Matías Zegers and José Luis Uribe Ortiz, in Santiago, Chile, on October 27, 2022. Recorded and transcribed document.

school of São Paulo and closer to the evocation of nature typical of the Carioca (Rio de Janeiro) school, her work creates an architecture of place through the austere use of materials, which allows it to be organically integrated with the environment. Her connection to the context and sensitivity to local demands distinguishes Juaçaba's work. In Casa Rio Bonito, thick side walls are built with edged stone, and four steel beams span them to support the roof and roof-deck. The formal language contrasts the archaic with the contemporary, smooth with rough, full with empty, and opaque with transparent. "In the case of Casa Rio Bonito, I was on site with the master builder," Juaçaba said. "A man who took care of everything and taught me everything. So why would I be drawing for him? It would not make sense. He already knows everything, so he drew it for me. It is completely related to the type of construction I am proposing." Juaçaba expresses confidence in the craft, intuition, and reverse processes that characterize her creative and collaborative approach to building.

In Ecuador, architect Daniel Moreno Flores, with French architect Marie Combette, founded La Cabina de la Curiosidad, an enthusiastic and creative studio where different scales of work are addressed. The architects introduce

Above and opposite page: La Cabina de la Curiosidad, Hospedaje en la Cantera, Baños de Agua Santa, Ecuador, 2022. Photos courtesy the architects.

everyday artifacts into interior spaces to promote domestic engineering. They are also interested in developing projects that stimulate public living, where the architectural object is configured with limited resources and using local labor. This is how, both in domestic interventions and in the architectural devices arranged in the territory, the architecture is sensitive to the inhabitant and to the environment. In design terms, La Cabina de la Curiosidad reacts almost instinctively to architectural problems, such as folding doors, moving a wall, or suspending a slab. As Moreno says:

All types of actions in a broad sense trigger questioning, activism, reflection, and the development of thought. Everything is a great opportunity to formulate hypotheses or particular systems. In the same vein, the presence of any object, event, or fact has a meaning. There is a very strong appreciation for and recognition of the work of an artisan, for the human activities carried out, for the resources, for the narrative of this combination and for the territory in which we find ourselves at every moment. On this path, there is a sensitivity in highlighting the crudeness of systems as entities capable of self-formulation.

In Paraguay, José Cubilla stands out for his deep commitment to local construction techniques, which has made him one of the most influential architects in the region. Along with Javier Corvalán and Solano Benítez, Cubilla's work is characterized by experimentation with various earth building

techniques, seen in a succession of architectural projects featuring rammed earth. Experiencia Luque (2003), Vivienda Takuru (2016), Edificio Valois (2021), and Vivienda Mirikina (2021) reflect a progressive design process, with each work informing the creative process of the next. With the humility of a potter, Cubilla orchestrates the movement of artisans whose corporeality become part of the process. It corresponds to a contemporary architecture work based on local construction traditions and a vernacular typology present in rural Paraguay. Regarding the vernacular architecture in Paraguay, the architect points out: "I fell in love with how people could understand the space so spontaneously, with such simple materials, where they could see how the space was lived. The high openings, the brick floors, the galleries, the intermediate spaces."[4] Cubilla values the rich spatial and constructive dimensions present in the anonymous architecture of Paraguay, which he adopts as a model to enrich his designs.

4. Excerpt of the conversation between José Cubilla and José Luis Uribe Ortiz, in Asunción, Paraguay, on October 8, 2019. Recorded and transcribed document.

After developing their disciplinary practice in Europe, Barclay & Crousse returned to Peru to apply all of the experience acquired in the old continent. As Jean Pierre Crousse has said: "In Europe, as in other industrialized regions, the project ends in the project, in the tender. Then there is an execution; there is control over the execution, but the creative process is over. Here, in South America, the construction process often ends after the work is finished and a little time has passed. So,

Above and opposite page: José Cubilla, Vivienda Mirikina, Mariano Roque Alonso, Paraguay, 2021. Photos courtesy the architect.

prolonging and having extra time to continue with this creative process around an architectural project is invaluable. It is an incredible advantage that we South Americans have."

One of Barclay & Crousse's most notable works is the Paracas Museum, whose exterior walls mediate between the daily life of the interior and the natural landscape. The work incorporates pozzolanic cement into its construction process, making the walls resistant to desert saltpeter. This gives the surface a rough, natural reddish color, which blends in with the neighboring hills. Its patina gives the building the appearance of ceramic, similar to the pre-Columbian Indigenous pottery exhibited inside.

After surveying this architectural diversity on the continent, it is possible to point to some commonalities. First, the defects associated with the artisanal crafting of material resources acquires value as an expression of South American architecture. The dripping of mortar and the patchworks of materials are features of architecture built by hand, providing roughness and vibration to the surfaces of walls, slabs, and floors. These qualities add value to the haptic dimension in each work's spatial routes, which is part of this architecture. The works' surfaces are exhibited with raw sincerity.

The geography of South America exudes a character from which an architectural culture can learn. It corresponds to an architecture of humility, which does not condition us to create a particular type of architecture but invites us to review how these architects operate in a constantly changing territory due to political, economic, climatic, health, and natural crises. It is in these areas of scarcity and restriction that architects invent. In this creative process, craftsmanship, through the local trades of bricklayers, carpenters, and stonemasons, has taken on a particular role.[5] Because South American architects cannot opt for high technology, the most economical human resource appears to be the craft of the artisan. Thus, due to the cultural and socioeconomic context in which South American architecture is framed, architects choose the technical rather than the technological.

In this context, South America provides a breeding ground for architectural practices inspired by contingent reality, which becomes a model for peripheral architecture around the world. It contributes to the diversity of approaches and perspectives necessary for the discipline, as seen in work by Studio Mumbai in India, Amateur Architecture Studio in China, and Kéré Architecture in Burkina Faso. Along with these practices, South American architecture constitutes a trench rather than an architectural scene – an architecture of resistance to the models established by globalization. South American architecture considered primitive, in Adrian Forty's sense of the term, for whom "primitive" does not denigrate what it describes[6] but bases its beauty on the "denigrated," is typical of architecture on the margins, built with a limited budget, and, in some cases, recycled materials, creating a contemporary architecture that values the local. While the practices here still require a deeper critical approach, they recognize an attitude that allows one to face the new scenarios offered by contemporaneity.

5. However, this constructive logic does not leave aside the exploration of contemporary materials associated with the artificiality of local production, such as the use of rubber from discarded tires. Material exploration raises new technological possibilities in architecture, but conditioned by the economy of resources available on the continent.

6. Adrian Forty, "Primitivo" La palabra y el concepto (Santiago: Ediciones ARQ, 2018), 9.

José Luis Uribe Ortiz holds a doctorate in architecture from the Universidad Politecnica de Madrid and is a professor at the School of Architecture of the Universidad de Talca, Chile. His books include *Talca, matter of education* (2013), *Against the Tide* (2016), and *Viaje a Paraguay* (2022). He also directed the film *Ugly, Dirty & Bad: A Contemporary Architecture in Latin America* (2022), and *Inhabiting the territory* (2023).

Barclay & Crousse, Museo del Sitio de la Cultura Paracas, Paracas, Peru, 2016.
Photos courtesy the architects.

During the Bolivian month-long celebration of Alasitas, miniatures of food, cars, people, money, houses, and of the Tiwanakan deity Ekeko (god of luck and prosperity, seen here in a red cap) are sold in marketplaces. The miniatures, which represent desires and ambitions for the coming year, are consecrated by both a Catholic and an Indigenous priest. Photo: Guido Alejo Mamani.

Guido Alejo Mamani

The Aymara Avant-garde

Understanding Andean cultures requires going back to the civilizational rupture of the pre-Hispanic world caused by Spanish colonization and, later, the transition to the republican era's institutional dynamics. In this region, the "Indigenous issue" is fundamental to understanding the historical tensions that derive from this rupture as in some cases it relates to the discursive essence of the state, and in others, it manifests as an obstacle to modernity.

Architecture is molded to collective cultural requirements and imaginaries. This is more visible in regions where the Indigenous population has transitioned from resistance and survival to autonomous and creative development. Such is the case of the Aymara population, who live on the outskirts of the cities of La Paz and El Alto, in Bolivia, located in an arid region more than 3,800 meters above sea level, and whose architecture has gained media attention in recent years.

The Historical Context

Pre-Hispanic Andean architecture was spectacular, showing diversity in urban and architectural conceptions and dispositions, with a common symbolic language, continuous use of the *chakana*,[1] and a profusion of color in buildings.[2] The European invasion marked an inflection point that truncated a centuries-long process of Indigenous artistic and cultural development, juxtaposing architectural styles more akin to European aesthetics with local expressions, thereby producing a loss of creative autonomy.

Colonialism started an ongoing process of subalternation of the pre-Hispanic population, now termed Indigenous, based on a system of hierarchized, ascending social strata.[3] This is reflected in the valuations of "mestizo" and "creole" architecture versus the "Indian." The "Indian-Indigenous" is, in many cases throughout the Andean region, marginalized or confined as a peripheral traditional work.

With independence, the creole and mestizo bourgeoisies of the new nations maintained the social structure of and affinity with the Spanish. However, with the consolidation of modern nation-states, nationalism and "Indigenism"

1. *Chakana* means "great shining light" in the Aymara and "bridge" in the Quechua. It is represented by a stepped symbol often called the "square cross" or "Andean cross."
2. In specific cases like the Puma Punku temple (Tiwanaku), the stone facade was covered with paint in different colors and gold plate.
3. Generally speaking, the strata ascend in social importance: the Indian (native), the mestizo (a mix of a native and creole), and the creole (a child of Spaniards born in the colonies).

promoted the revaluation of pre-Hispanic Indigenous aesthetics, though without considering their modern descendants. It is not surprising that, at the beginning of the 20th century, governments promoted architectural styles like Neo-Incan in Peru or Neo-Tiwanakan in Bolivia. Today, a process of accepting plurality and multiculturalism is underway, but the cultural elite still treat the Indigenous world as a vulnerable minority anchored to its past.

Bolivia has a particular condition: the majority of its population is Indigenous,[4] but the Indigenous population is still assumed to be marginal, poor, and lacking new creative potential. Until the late 19th century, these ideas were widespread, with the exploitation and/or indifference of local governments, famines, and epidemics that plagued the Aymara and Quechua.[5] It was normal to read newspaper headlines like "The Indian Race Is Mortally Wounded," illustrating the anticipation of the Indigenous population's disappearance.

However, the "Indian" has demonstrated great resilience and resistance, playing a leading role in many of Bolivia's historical political processes, often against the wishes of the intellectual establishment. The 20th century witnessed the social reconfiguration of the Indigenous world due to migrations, greater penetration of capitalism in these communities, and adaptation to global dynamics and economic informality.[6] This represented significant changes in lifestyles, social relations, and cultural expressions. The outskirts of La Paz and El Alto are emblematic in this regard.

From Andean Periphery to Creative Laboratory

In the mid-20th century, the Aymara population, driven by poverty and precarity, left the Altiplano and migrated en masse to La Paz, a process that intensified toward the end of the century, populating large areas on the periphery. This is one of the origins of El Alto, a suburb, located 4,150 meters above sea level, that claimed its autonomy in 1980 in the face of abandonment by the La Paz government.

As a result, the migrant population's houses were self-built, implying the continuity of rural housing, with its community relations and rituals. The rural function of the house remains unchanged in the urban context: to live and produce, supporting an informal economy in which the house must contribute to the family's economic subsistence. During this process, the Aymara population differentiated and categorized three architectural typologies: the "uta," the "atusa," and the "edificio."

4. In the 2001 Population and Housing Census, 62 percent of the Bolivian population identified as belonging to an Indigenous group.
5. The Aymara and Quechua nations are historically the largest population group in Bolivia.
6. Bolivia has the highest percentage of economic informality in the world, which even influences cultural dynamics.

An uta in the Alto Lima neighborhood of El Alto. The material shift from adobe to brick is a sign of the accelerated changes in the city. All photos: Guido Alejo Mamani.

The Urban Uta

Uta means housing in the Aymara. In the urban uta, design and conception guidelines were maintained according to rural Aymara architectural forms. The spatial layout included open spaces (courtyards) for socialization and agricultural production, surrounded by rooms that multiply as the family grows. Later, spaces were converted for economic and commercial use. It was made of adobe and rammed earth and other earth construction techniques, as well as other locally available materials. The uta was used widely until the 1990s.

The Altusa

Altusa is a portmanteau of the Spanish *alto*, or tall, and the Aymara *uta*. The altusas were blocks of two- or three-story buildings facing the street. The ground floor was generally intended for generating income. The rest of the lot maintained the characteristics of the uta – that is, a courtyard surrounded by adjoining rooms. The altusas were built with adobe. Over time, concrete structures and bricks were incorporated. Many altusas have decorated facades, implying a certain distinction. Their construction was prolific from the 1960s to the 1990s.

The Edificio

In the urban Aymara language, the Spanish term *edificio* is used differently from altusa, distinguishing its height, materials, and construction techniques. The use of earth as a building material is abandoned in favor of brick and concrete, technology already employed by the Indigenous bourgeoisie in La Paz in the mid-20th century.

This architectural type spread through popular, economically vibrant neighborhoods in the second half of the 20th

Various altusas in El Alto. The decoration of these constructions often includes elements such as the chakana, which becomes more profuse in later styles.

7. *Cholet* is a play on words from *chalet* and *cholo*: a cholet is a chalet made by *cholos*, a term for "hicks." The term *cholet* is used pejoratively to differentiate it from academic architecture.
8. *Qamiri* is colloquially used to name Aymaras with more material possessions but who maintain close ties with their community.
9. I delve into the effects of socioeconomic inequality present in contemporary Andean architecture in Guido Alejo, "Aproximaciones a las dimensiones de la desigualdad desde la arquitectura de la vivienda paceña y alteña," *Revista Umbrales* 40 (August 2023): 17–46.

century, parallel to the altusa, and remains relevant to this day. It is the basis for contemporary architecture pejoratively called "cholet,"[7] which is defined by facade work and public socialization spaces that seek prestige and differentiation.

Contemporary Architecture of the Qamiri

In a historical process that surpasses survival conditions to achieve relative economic stability, the *qamiri*[8] ("rich people" in the Aymara) become notable for the spectacularism of their buildings.[9] The qamiri adopt elements from different cultures, especially from China, in a utilitarian manner. There is a rivalry for prestige with other qamiri through parties and architecture. Their leadership is not necessarily political but cultural and economic, as many of their expressions are followed in the popular sphere.

To some extent, the emergence of the qamiri implies
the return of a lost, pre-Hispanic elite who were subsumed
and nearly exterminated during the colonial era but became
assimilated and alienated in the republican era. Today, a new
Aymara elite, which quietly reinvented itself during the 20th
century, fills the void of architecture clientele that the mestizo and creole bourgeoisie did not want to occupy.

Their architecture adopts the edificio typology, which is
clad with materials and colors that imply social differentiation
and prestige, with the main ambition being aesthetic symbolism. Initially, the qamiri production was communal. Owners,
masons, and architects contributed to the design of the building, outside of the academic canons and without the need for
government validation. Currently, construction companies
and renowned architects/builders have been consolidated.

10. My essay, "El Alto" delves into the aesthetic aspect based on figures and maps in the city of El Alto. See Guido Alejo, "El Alto: la reconfiguración de los imaginarios a través de la estética," (blog), June 8, 2022, https://guidoalejo. wordpress.com/2022/06/08/el-alto-la-reconfiguracion-de-los-imaginarios-a-traves-de-la-estetica/.

There are five aesthetic variants in cholets,[10] whose names are not necessarily commonly used but which I propose as categories for classification:

Geometric
This aesthetic variant is based on representations of intricate geometric figures, often around the openings in the building. It is one of the oldest aesthetic variants, present in old rural altusas, readapted in the '90s, and still in use today.

Eclectic Historicism
This variant is inspired by the architecture of various parts of the world and different epochs, from Arabia and China to the Gothic and neoclassical Europe. It was widespread in the late '90s and early 21st century. Today it is less common.

Andean
Inspired by pre-Hispanic Andean expressions, especially the Tiwanaku culture, the most used iconography is the chakana and stepped iconography. Although pre-Hispanic motifs were present in the altusas in the past, now architects like Miguel Prieto, in the '90s, and Freddy Mamani are their main promoters. This category is currently in a process of reinvention, incorporating other contemporary elements of Andean culture such as elements of folk dances.

Polychrome Minimalism
This recent variant is promoted by academic architects. Its design and polychromy are so intricate that, in essence, it ceases to be minimalist even though it is often called such. Currently, it is in the process of diffusion.

Futurist
This represents elements associated with the contemporary, particularly high-tech elements and machinery such as circuit boards, nuts, and metal structures. This category also incorporates representations of science-fiction characters and Western pop culture. One of the architects who promoted this aesthetic was Santos Churata (who died in 2021). It became more visible in the 2010s.

Aesthetic Dynamics and Historical Process
Aesthetic dynamics usually correspond to historical-cultural junctures that influence the collective imaginations of the population. In the context of contemporary qamiri

architecture, aesthetics tends to be secondary in relation to other architectural elements, such as the function of housing and ritual.

The geometric aesthetic was one of the first to develop in the rural-urban migration. The historicist eclectic aesthetic had its heyday when urban architectural references were sought in the 1980s and '90s. However, by the late '90s, the Andean aesthetic underwent greater development during a political moment of cultural reaffirmation and social struggles that sought ethnic and popular vindication (2000–03).[11] Andean style was a strong architectural expression until the late 2010s.

With the overcoming of extreme poverty and the rising visibility of middle and upper classes of Aymara origin, the adoption of an aesthetic promoted by academia began, such as minimalism, whose persistence corresponds to a sense of prestige,[12] with excessive polychromy and shapes representing a kind of negotiation or borrowing between academic ideas inspired by both the Global North and local culture. In the last decade, high-tech representations in architecture have increased due to the diverse interpretations of the "modern,"[13] but from a futuristic approach, in line with other phenomena in urban Aymara society, such as the emergence of young people skilled in artisanal robotics – a semi-industrialized production of electronic components – and direct relationships with technologically advanced countries like those in the West and China. The futuristic aesthetic is in vogue for the most opulent buildings.

Urban Aymara culture tends to take contemporary global elements and incorporate them into its architectural repertoire without radically changing them. These are temporary borrowings that will be replaced in the future, according to the focused investment in prestige and more strategic social relations.

Identity in Urban Aymara Architecture

Identity, understood as the set of stable characteristics of a society that is differentiated from another and in a continuous process of self-affirmation, is not necessarily determined by aesthetics, materials, or construction technologies, at least in the urban Aymara context present on the outskirts of La Paz and in El Alto. This identity is linked to three core elements:

1. The dual function of the Aymara dwelling as living and producing is present in the different architectural typologies throughout its history. Generally, the production spaces are

11. This moment corresponds to the prelude of the so-called Gas War in which El Alto played a leading role in articulating a discourse of strong cultural reaffirmation, later enriched by other ideas. This political struggle led to the promulgation of a new constitution in 2009, making Bolivia a plurinational state.

12. Traditionally, for much of academia, the architecture produced by the West sets a standard to follow, often contrary to trends emerging from the popular sphere.

13. Apart from the historiography of modern Western architecture and the social sciences that interpret modernity from a structural perspective, in the Andes, the term *modern* has a particular association with contemporary, quality infrastructure and high technology.

Opposite page, from top: Two buildings in El Alto exemplify the Geometric aesthetic variant. An Eclectic Historicism building in El Alto draws on Arabian architectural motifs. Two buildings, one in La Paz (left) and one in El Alto, use pre-Hispanic Andean aesthetic expressions. Above, from top: Two buildings in El Alto exemplify the Polychrome Minimalist aesthetic. Two buildings in El Alto draw on Western pop culture (Iron Man, for example) and science fiction to produce a Futurist aesthetic.

Marketplace in El Alto during the festival of Alasitas.

on the ground floor of the building, with the living spaces set above. The facade is intended to produce prestige as well as social differentiation.

2. Andean societies maintain part of their pre-Columbian worldview and philosophy.[14] The dwelling is conceived as an element of continuous reciprocity, especially with Pachamama,[15] to whom offerings are made when starting construction, when pouring the first slab, and upon completion. The house is also celebrated annually on carnival Tuesdays in a ceremony called "ch'alla," as a sign of gratitude.

3. The dwelling is conceived as a subject and treated as a living entity that is part of the urban and cultural environment, part of a reciprocal relationship with a strong sense of locality, and which is thanked and celebrated for providing shelter and sustenance.

Architecture as Avant-garde

The term *avant-garde* is used here to refer to an architecture that is not only the most representative of several architectural processes of popular origin but is also essentially a cultural element that has transcended to the symbolic and ritual level, marking a social horizon and its future possibilities. Architecture in Andean rituality is part of a worldview rooted in pre-Hispanic traditions. One of these traditions is the month-long celebration of the Alasitas festival that starts January 24, essentially marking the popular desires and aspirations with miniatures that represent life goals to be achieved.

The miniature house of the Alasitas festival is mostly a symbolic reference to desired achievements. The miniatures of the Alasitas festival also correspond to the current architectural aesthetics dynamics, showcasing buildings that enjoy social recognition and correlate with major urban trends, marking them as avant-garde in a cultural and ritualistic sense.

Another element marking them as avant-garde is their dissemination and convergence with popular regional architecture in the new urban reality of Bolivia. Migration within the country has greatly transformed the urban image of small cities as well as metropolises, transgressing conservative stances on urban identities that were assumed to be Indigenous.

Most of the outskirts and new urban centers feature buildings analogous to the edificio, with a living-producing function, brick and concrete structure, and a colorful facade. This convergence implies close relationships and cultural continuities, especially between the Aymara and Quechua populations.

14. I explore this in Guido Alejo, "Bolivia: Arquitectura y Ritualidad, Implicancias de las Miniaturas de Edificios en la Festividad de la Alasita," *London Journal of Research in Humanities and Social Sciences* 24, no. 4 (2024): 75–89.
15. Pachamama is Mother Earth, who collaborates and provides sustenance.

Panorama of contemporary architecture in El Alto.

Being avant-garde is not necessarily an exclusive condition of an enlightened minority but can be a movement in which multiple contributions converge, in some cases individual, in many cases communal, with such influence and universalization that they feed back into historical changes in a society autonomously forging its future.

Implications

More than 100 years ago, Bolivian elites predicted the disappearance of the "Indian," as was the case in much of South and North America. However, today, in the Andes, the presence of the Indigenous is undeniable. A civilization has reinvented itself amid neglect and informality, losing part of its cultural repertoire along the way but preserving its cultural core and adopting foreign elements in a utilitarian manner. In the Andes, these processes are known as *pachakuti*: the transformation of everything. The Andes are dynamic; their culture can be nostalgic but also curious and eager for experimentation in an ever-changing and challenging world.

Guido Alejo Mamani is an Aymara Alteño architect and an independent researcher, essayist, and columnist based in El Alto, Bolivia.

Women Architects Awarded at the Panamerican Architecture Biennial of Quito 1994 to 2022

The Architecture Biennial of Quito (BAQ) started in 1978, but it became Panamerican in its ninth edition (1994). Since then, it has established itself as one of the most important biennials in the world through its awards and academic and cultural agenda, disseminating architectural design practice and theory to a broader audience. This visual article analyzes the Panamerican awards, focusing on built works from a gender perspective that identifies the award-winning projects designed by women.

A *project by* **Mariana Alves Barbosa**

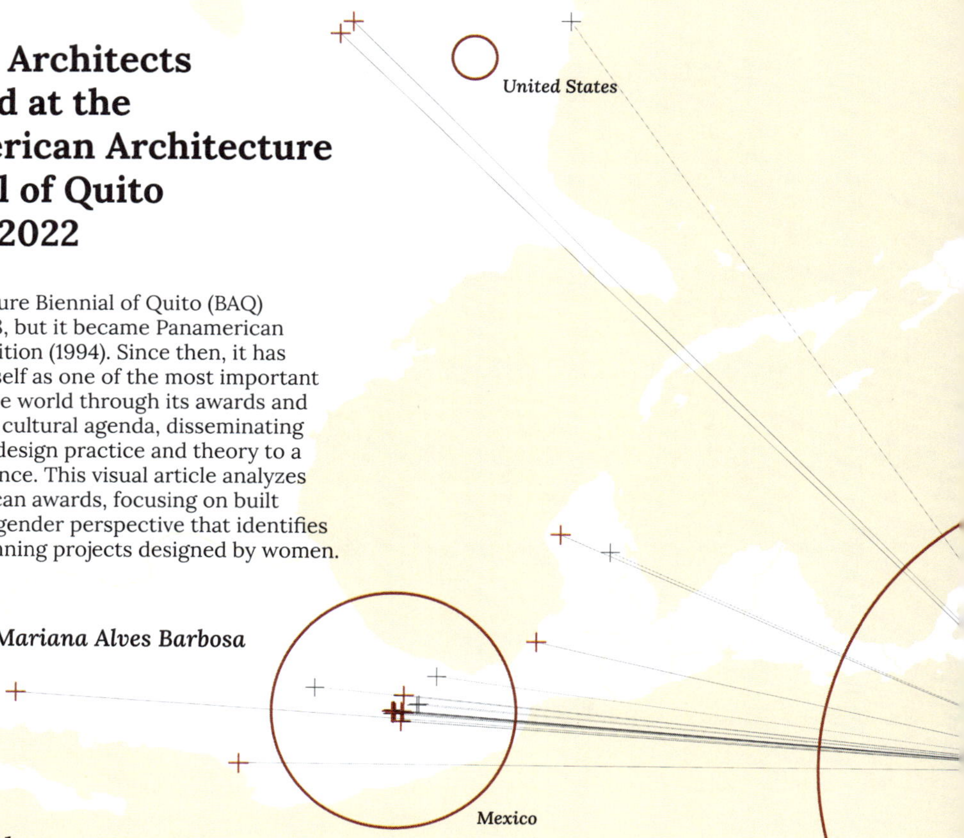

United States

Mexico

Map Legend

Cross = Georeferencing of each project awarded by the BAQ

 Awarded projects designed by women architects, 70 projects

Awarded projects designed by men or undefined authorship*, 107 projects

*6 projects did not have their authorship defined.

- - - - Award-winning projects outside America (Germany, Philippines, South Africa, and Spain)

Size of Ring = Total projects designed by women architects awarded by the BAQ per country

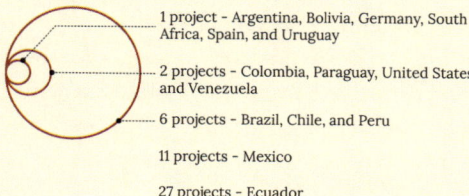

1 project - Argentina, Bolivia, Germany, South Africa, Spain, and Uruguay

2 projects - Colombia, Paraguay, United States, and Venezuela

6 projects - Brazil, Chile, and Peru

11 projects - Mexico

27 projects - Ecuador

Map Spots = Contextual information

 Andes Mountains   Amazon Basin

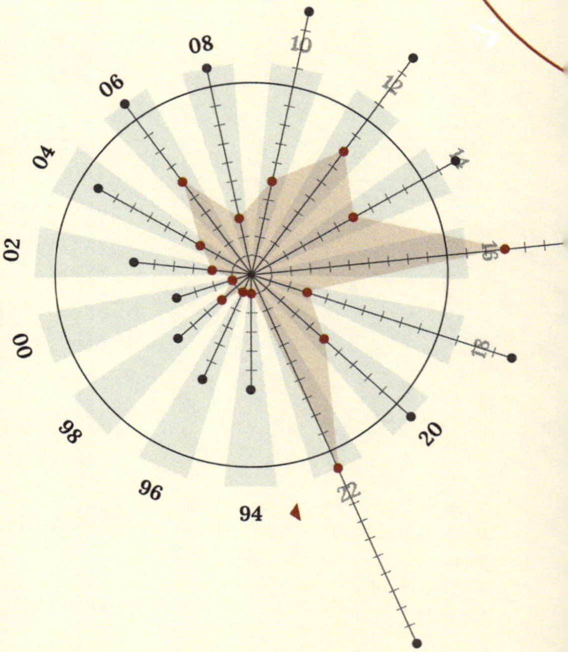

Data source:
*https://arquitecturapanamericana.com
and catalogs from https://issuu.com/bienalquito*

08 10 06 12 04 14 02 16 00 18 98 20 96 94 22

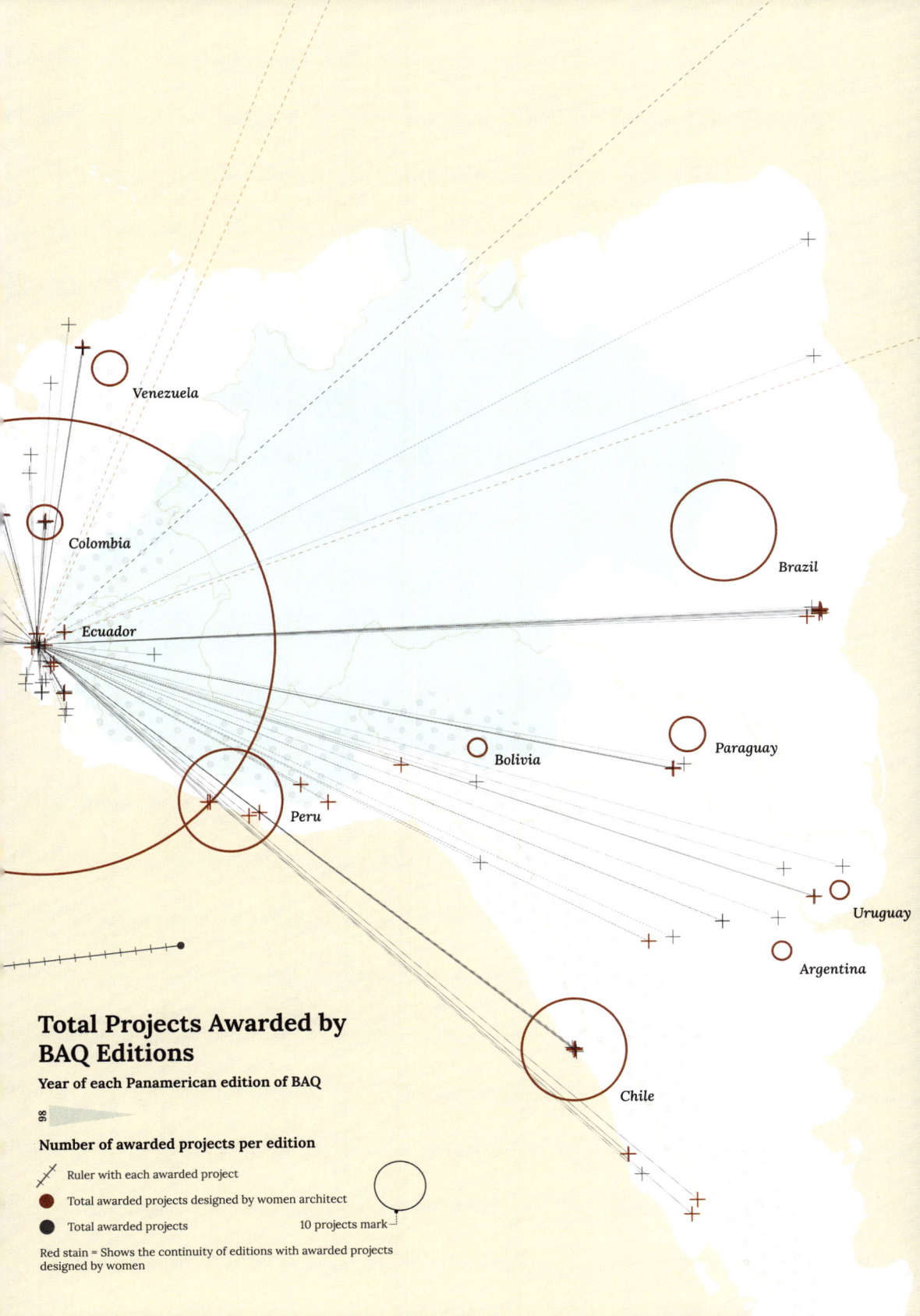

Venezuela

Colombia

Brazil

Ecuador

Paraguay

Bolivia

Peru

Uruguay

Argentina

Total Projects Awarded by BAQ Editions

Year of each Panamerican edition of BAQ

Chile

98

Number of awarded projects per edition

Ruler with each awarded project

Total awarded projects designed by women architect

Total awarded projects

10 projects mark

Red stain = Shows the continuity of editions with awarded projects designed by women

Awarded Projects Designed by Women Architects in BAQ Editions

The BAQ offers different types of awards. The titles, as well as the intentions of the awards, change over the years, but they can be summarized as: Biennial Grand Prix, International or World Award, Panamerican Award, National Award, and awards by categories. The National Award is dedicated exclusively to Ecuadorian projects, guaranteeing recognition for the country's architecture.

1994 EDITION

1. Remodelación de un Sector del Convento de Santo Domingo
Ecuador, 1992
Marcela Alemán, Patrick de Sutter
National Award

1996 EDITION

2. Casa Samaniego Coloma
Ecuador, 1996
Roberto Moscoso Cevallos, María Samaniego Ponce, Adrián Moreno Nuñez
National Award

1998 EDITION

3. Casa en Lago Pirihueico
Chile, 1996
Mirene Elton, Mauricio Léniz
Biennial Grand Prix

Photo courtesy the architects.

4. Museo de la Ciudad
Ecuador, 1998
José Ordóñez, Francisco Naranjo, Lucia Vásconez
National Award

2000 EDITION

5. Centro Cultural Metropolitano
Ecuador, 2000
Fernando Flores González, Jaime Andrade Haymann, Soledad Dulce Figueroa, Mauricio Moreno Vintimilla
International or World Award

2002 EDITION

6. Jardins Parque Industrial Flextronics
Brazil, 2000
Lucia Porto, Sidonio Porto
Landscape Architecture

7. Memorial de los Detenidos Desaparecidos
Uruguay, 1998
Ruben Otero, Martha Kohen

Photo courtesy the architects.

2004 EDITION

8. Habilitación Urbana San Rafael Barrio Unido
Venezuela, 2004
Marines Pocaterra, Isabel Pocaterra, Silvia Soonets, Victor Gastier
International or World Award

9. Parque de la Juventud Carandiru
Brazil, 2004
Rosa Grena Kliass
International or World Award

Photo: Nelson Kon.

10. Parque Lineal Machángara
Ecuador, 2004
Manuel Uribe, Patrício Guayasamín, María Belén Gudiño, Patricio Hidalgo Carrera
National Award

2006 EDITION

11. Student Lounges at The University of Michigan
United States, 2006
Karen M'Closkey, Keith VanDerSys
International or World Award

12. Plaza Mies Van der Rohe
United States, 2005
Karen M'Closkey, Keith VanDerSys
International or World Award

13. Casa de las Artes San Lucas
Ecuador, 2006
Daniela Mora Ordóñez
National Award

2008 EDITION

14. Museo Provincial de Bellas Artes Emilio Caraffa
Argentina, 2008
Sara Gramática, Jorge Morini, José Pisani, Eduardo
Urtubey, Lucio Morini

Photo: Gonzalo Viramonte.

**15. Construcción de 16 Viviendas de Quincha Mejorada
Modular Para Damnificados del Terremoto**
Peru, 2007
María Eugenia Lacarra Córdova

16. Inkwenkwezi Secondary School
South Africa, 2007
Jo Noero, Heinrich Wolff, Sonja Petrus Spamer

17. Plaza Víctor J. Cuesta
Ecuador, 2008
Javier Durán, María Augusta Hermida
National Award

18. Restauración Convento de San Francisco
Bolivia, 2004
Fidel Cossio Zapata, Patricia Vasquez Aguilera

2010 EDITION

19. Parque las Américas
Chile, 2007
Teodoro Fernández Larrañaga, Paulina Curard Délano,
Sebastián Hernández Silva, Danilo Martic Vukasovic

20. Borde Urbano del Jardín Botánico de Medellín
Colombia, 2007
Ana Elvira Vélez, Lorenzo Castro

21. Programa Habitacional Paraisópolis de Brasil
Brazil, 2010
Edson Elito, Joana Fernandes, Cristiane Otsuka Takiy

22. Casa Cruz
Ecuador, undated
Pablo Moreira, Natalia Corral, Rubén Moreira, Yadhira
Álvarez, Milton Chávez
National Award

23. Parque do Belém, Tatuapé
Brazil, undated
Alessandra Gizela da Silva, Apoena Amaral, José Luiz
Brenna
Panamerican Award

24. Escuela de Artes Plásticas de Oaxaca
Mexico, 2008
Mauricio Rocha, Gabriela Carrillo, Carlos Facio, Rafael
Carrillo, Silvana Jourdan
Biennial Grand Prix

Photo: Rafael Carrillo.

25. Fundación Teletón Sede Central
Paraguay, 2010
Solano Benítez, Gloria Cabral, Cristina Cabrera

Photo: Federico Cairoli.

26. Edificio Habitacional Gen
Chile, 2010
Felipe Assadi, Francisca Pulido

Photo: Sergio Pirrone.

2012 EDITION

27. Plaza Santa Clara
Ecuador, 2011
Boris Albornoz, Rodrigo Donoso, José Luis
Flores, Marco Gonzáles, Gabriela Luna, Sebastián
Naranjo, Andrea Ortíz, Andrés Regalado
National Award and Urban Landscape Architecture

**28. Mejora de Viviendas rurales en el Valle
del Colca**
Peru, 2010
José Carrión Carrillo, Juan De la Serna Torroba,
Jorge Luis Chávez Marroquín, Fiorela Cano
Quintanilla, Rocío Cayllahua Yucra y Jessica María
Dulanto Martínez
Social Habitat and Development

29. Residencial Parque Novo Santo Amaro V
Brazil, 2012
Héctor Vigliecca, Luciene Quel, Neli Shimizu,
Ronald Werner Fiedler, Caroline Bertoldi, Kelly
Bozzato, Pedro Ichimaru, Bianca Riotto, Mayara
Rocha Christ, Fábio Pittas, Thaísa Fróes, Aline
Ollertz, Sérgio Faraulo, Paulo Serra, Luci Maie

**30. Ladrillos, Bloques y Otros Elementos
Abandonados y Parches**
Ecuador, 2012
David Barragán, Pascual Gangotena, Marialuisa
Borja y Esteban Benavides
National Award and Rehabilitation and Recycling

Photo: Kliwadenko Novas.

2014 EDITION

31. Torno Co. Lab.
Ecuador, 2014
Carolina Rodas, Felipe Donoso, Carla Chávez
National Award

32. Leyva 506
Mexico, 2014
Lilian Rebollo Uribe, Edgar Saúl Bahena Cruz
International or World Award

33. Memorial a las Víctimas de la Violencia
Mexico, 2013
Julio Gaeta, Luby Springall, Ricardo López
International or World Award

34. Casa Albergue
Ecuador, 2012
Pablo Moreira, Natalia Corral, Ruben Moreira,
Yadhira Alvarez, Milton Chavez
International or World Award

35. Escuela en Chuquibambilla
Peru, 2014
Paulo Afonso, Marta Maccaglia, Ignacio Bosch,
Borja Bosch
International or World Award

Photo courtesy the architects.

36. Parklets São Paulo
Brazil, 2012
Guilherme Ortenblad, Kathleen, Chiang, Mariane
Christovam, Ana Carolina de Lima, Alex Ninomia,
Luana Pedrosa, Tadeu Omae
International or World Award

2016 EDITION

**37. Rehabilitación del ex Hotel Colonial para
Conjunto Habitacional**
Ecuador, 2015
Rubén Moreira, Natalia Corral, Yadhira Álvarez,
Pablo Moreira, Milton Chávez
National Award

38. Carlota
Ecuador, 2016
Verónica Reed
National Award

39. Oficinas de Publicidad Fahrenheit DDB
Peru, 2015
Peter Seinfeld, María Paz Ballén
International or World Award

**40. 1100 – Sistema de Equipamientos
Comunitarios**
Venezuela, 2016
Gabriel Visconti, Ana Morales, Laura Di Benedetto,
Rolando Campos, Stevenson Piña, Marcos Coronel
International or World Award

Photo courtesy the architects.

41. Foto Museo Cuatro Caminos
Mexico, 2015
Mauricio Rocha, Gabriela Carrillo
International or World Award

42. Parque de los Algarrobos
Ecuador, 2016
Esteban Jaramillo, Christine Van Sluys
National Award

43. Intervención Urbano Arquitectónica Campus Central Universidad de Cuenca
Ecuador, 2016
Javier Durán Aguilar, Juan Carvallo Ochoa, Ivan Sinchi Toral, Cristian Sotomayor Bustos, Isabel Carrasco Vintimilla, Kabir Monteisnos
National Award

44. Patio Fresnos
Mexico, 2014
Jorge Ambrosi, Gabriela Etchegaray
International or World Award

45. Mapocho 42k_Promenade Geografica para la Equidad Social
Chile, 2016
Sandra Iturriaga, Paulina Ibieta, Francisco Croxatto, Juan Baixas, Juana Zunino
International or World Award

46. Museo Arqueológico y Centro Cultural de Orellana
Ecuador, 2016
Rubén Moreira, Natalia Corral, Yadhira Álvarez, Pablo Moreira, Milton Chávez
National Award

47. Biblioteca de Ciencias e Ingeniería Pucp
Peru, 2014
Patricia Llosa, Rodolfo Cortegana
International or World Award

48. Casa Gabriela
Mexico, 2015
Carlos Patrón Ibarra, Alejandro Patrón Sansor, Ana Patrón Ibarra, Estefanía Rivero Jansen
International or World Award

49. Museo de Sitio, Cultura Paracas
Peru, 2016
Jean Pierre Crousse, Sandra Barclay
International or World Award

Photo courtesy the architects.

2018 EDITION

50. Casa de las Camas en el Aire
Ecuador, 2017
Pascual Gangotena, David Barragán, Marialuisa Borja, Esteban Benavides
National Award

51. Ausbauhaus Neukölln
Germany, 2014
Henri Praeger, Jana Richter
International or World Award

52. Parque Lineal Ferrocarril de Cuernavaca: Primer Tramo
Mexico, 2017
Julio Gaeta, Luby Springall
International or World Award

2020 EDITION

53. Estudio Iturbide
Mexico, 2017
Mauricio Rocha, Gabriela Carrillo
Panamerican Award

54. Cacmu Verde. Cooperativa de Ahorro y Crédito Mujeres Unidas
Ecuador, 2019
Jorge Andrade Benítez, Gabriela Naranjo Serrano, Emilio Thodes Miranda, María José Valdospinos
Panamerican Award

Photo: Bicubik.

55. 8111
Colombia, 2018
Daniel Bonilla, Marcela Albornoz
Panamerican Award

Photo: Alejandro Arango.

56. Casa Hilo
Mexico, 2019
Cristoph Zeller, Ingrid Moye
Panamerican Award

57. Sinagoga Uhp
Paraguay, 2019
Horacio Cherniavskiy, Viviana Pozzoli
Panamerican Award

2022 EDITION

58. Casa De Música
Mexico, 2021
Gabriela Carrillo, Eric Valdez, Israel Espín, José
Amozurrutia, Carlos Facio
Biennial Grand Prix

Photo: Yoshihiro Koitani.

59. Teatro Regional Bio Bio
Chile, 2018
Smiljan Radic, Maria Gabriela Medrano Viteri,
Eduardo Castillo
Biennial Grand Prix

60. Muelle de San Blas
Mexico, 2022
Gabriela Carrillo, Eric Valdez, Israel Espín, José
Amozurrutia, Carlos Facio, Sofía Pavón, Roberto
Rosales, Abraham Espíndola
Panamerican Award

61. Casa con Patio
Chile, 2019
Guillermo Hevia García, Catalina Poblete
Panamerican Award

62. Residencias Villanueva
Ecuador, 2021
Fernanda Esquetini, Pablo Puente Rodríguez
National Award

63. Arrachay
Ecuador, 2020
Javier Mera Luna, María Beatriz Moncayo, Lesly
Jordania Villagrán
National Award

64. Casa los Nidos del Cholán
Ecuador, 2022
Marie Combette, Daniel Moreno Flores
National Award

65. Casa Pitaya
Ecuador, 2020
José María Saez, Florencia Sobrero, Martín Real
Buenaño
National Award

66. San Tola
Ecuador, 2022
Florencia Sobrero, Martín Real Buenaño
National Award

**67. Polideportivo y Ordenación Interior de
Manzana en el Turó de la Peira**
Spain, 2018
Anna Noguera, Javier Fernández

**68. Hospedajes en la Cantera, Viendo al
Tungurahua**
Ecuador, 2022
Marie Combette, Daniel Moreno Flores
National Award

Photo: Bicubik.

The projects that were not nominated for the
prize were awarded by category. Projects 27 and
30 received two awards each, making a total of 70
award-winning projects designed by women.

Mariana Alves Barbosa is an architect, researcher and professor. She cofounded the ARQTETATLAS Collective, a group that maps contemporary architecture by Latin American women. She is a course coordinator at the Institute of Architects of Brazil – São Paulo department (IABsp), where she is also coordinating the 26th IABsp Awards.

Alejandra Celedón

In and Out

The work of Chilean architects oscillates between two seemingly antagonistic impulses: pushing outward and pulling inward. These opposing forces expand or contract the boundaries of architecture. Between their interior and exterior margins, the local scene is divided between practices that have shrunk the discipline into self-referential exercises – to the point of risking sociocultural insignificance – and those that have stretched and diverted it to serve other agendas, such as the social, the political, or the environmental – allowing architecture to be influenced, even subsumed by other realms. These centrifugal and centripetal movements have written a double story of fiction and friction; they have also created a fertile ground for experimentation and new practices that have deepened and widened disciplinary limits. Some of the works that cemented Chilean architecture's international reputation belong to the first group: projects that test the discipline's autonomy, focusing on architecture as a refined, self-contained art form. Chile's constitutional debates following the social uprising, in 2019, and an increasing awareness of environmental crises brought to the surface since the pandemic have raised new, pressing questions over such modes of practice. In the face of our transformative moment, some previously celebrated works now seem conspicuously silent.

Inside

The "inward impulse" reinforces the idea that architecture begins and ends in buildings' spatial and formal possibilities. This perspective is a rare privilege: an approach perpetuated today by young architects but that was heavily promoted by previous generations. Some of these older examples appear in the compilation book *Blanca Montaña* (2008).[1] According to its editor, Miquel Adrià, "Chilean architecture is the most interesting and original of the entire American continent." This volume presents an overview of more than 100 works in which "geographies" and "biographies" prevail along formal and geometric explorations, set against an idyllic background. The book's title emphasizes the country's landscape, a constructed narrative that still guides the practice of many

1. Miquel Adrià, ed., *White Mountain: Recent Architecture in Chile / Blanca Montaña, Arquitectura en Chile* (Santiago: Ediciones Puro Chile, 2008).

Above and opposite page: Pezo von Ellrichshausen, Casa Luna, Yungay, Chile, 2022. Images courtesy the architects.

renowned Chilean architects. Likewise, the first architecture magazines dedicated to Chile instrumentalized this territorial rhetoric in relation to supposed poetics to which architecture responds. *Arquitectura Viva* 85: Último Chile (2002) began with a commentary by editor Luis Fernández-Galiano: "Chile is a geographical oxymoron. From the desert to the floes, this endless country slithers by the meridian to reconcile fire and ice, sliding between the Andes and the Pacific." In *Blanca Montaña*, the type of projects published (vacation homes, tourist buildings, restaurants, and new centers for private universities), with their obvious financial conditions (few restrictions), located in isolated contexts (whether on the Pacific coast or in the Andes Mountains at the end of the world), promoted a formula for Chilean architecture: a square white sheet of paper with sharp and abstract edges. In this centripetal movement, Casa Luna, designed and completed in 2022 by Pezo von Ellrichshausen, is perhaps its ultimate epitome.

Located at the foothills of the Andes Mountains, near the town of Yungay, Casa Luna – the architects' residence – is close enough to Chile's capital to be accessible but far enough away to make a one-day visit impractical. Moreover, its authors control its public presence in images. Visitors are not allowed to take photos, which means that the circulation

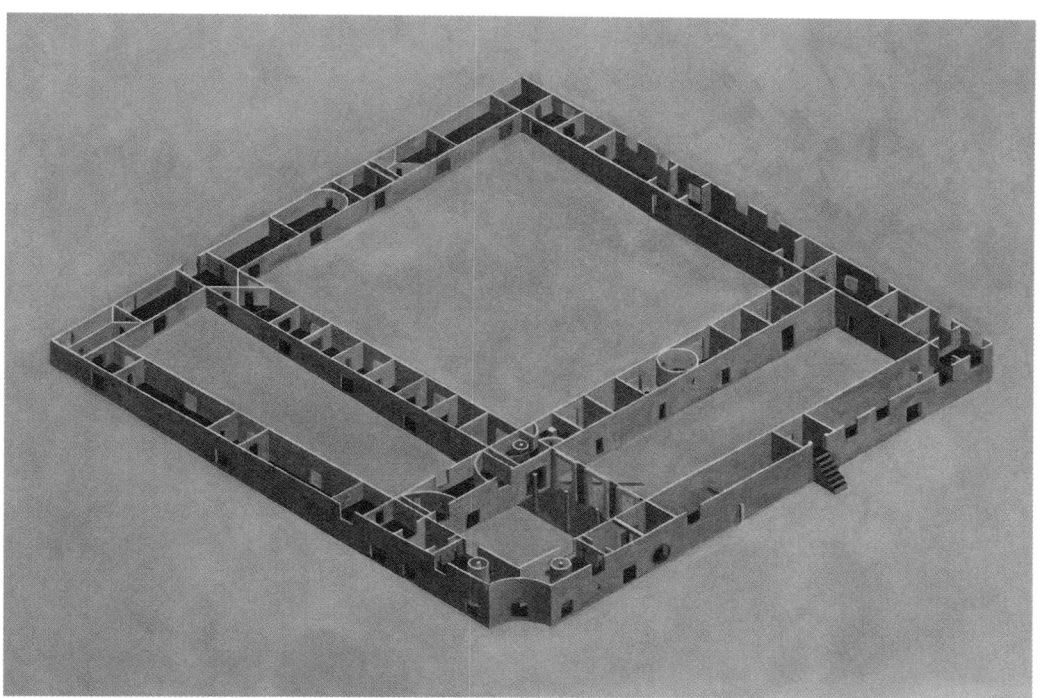

of images of the house is controlled by the architects (and their designated photographers). The house responds to the desire and degree of how it wants to be shown, a carefully managed representation of itself. Casa Luna is so inaccessible that its material existence is almost nil in comparison to its mediatic presence.

At almost 26,000 square feet and located on a 120-hectare estate, the house could be in Yungay or in any other corner of the world. The name Casa Luna comes from an unrecognizable reference to a local Chilean tradition: the architects claim that the size of its main courtyard follows that of a *medialuna*, or "half-moon," a typical enclosure in rodeos. However, the house's formal abstraction and monumentality seem to dispel any direct reference to rural history or local culture. Isolated like a monastery and self-contained like a cloister, Casa Luna reinforces a desire for autonomy through a rigorously square plan that frames four well-defined courtyards: a main square, two secondary rectangles, and a smaller square. The courtyards contain native trees and vegetation that, together with several fountains of different sizes, reinforce the idea of a microcosm outside of the world. Made of concrete, its mono-material execution contributes to a ruinous aesthetic. Freely growing weeds, ruderal plants, and wildflowers convey the image of carefully designed abandonment.

2. Javier Abio, "Casa Luna, la vivienda fortaleza de Pezo von Ellrichshausen," *Neo2*, August 28, 2023, https://www.neo2.com/casa-luna-pezo-von-ellrichshausen/.
3. Pezo von Ellrichshausen's cultural institution Fundacion Artificial is listed as the client of many of their projects.

Opposite page: A rectangular courtyard with a water feature is a microcosm seemingly apart from the world. Inside, the board-formed concrete records the texture of the vertical and horizontal wood formwork. Photos courtesy the architects.

The width of the rooms is uniform throughout the project. Instead of a corridor plan, the house has an enfilade configuration through which the rooms are connected sequentially. This gregarious spatial organization is more typical of the premodern era. The widely published axonometric of the project depicts the house as a sort of box of chocolates with rooms of different sizes and singular extruded shapes. Some of the rooms open onto the courtyards while others are enclosed, creating interiors enveloped by thick walls. Some rooms are crossed by diagonals; others by curved walls that randomly defy geometric rigidity. Casa Luna is always description and scarcely instruction. Rather than offering clarity about its use or function, it seems to be a detailed depiction of itself as an object to be contemplated but never apprehended.

A review described the house as an example of the "brutalist sensibility" that characterizes Pezo von Ellrichshausen's work: a "monolith on the edge of a cliff" whose "severe geometric profile" allows "rawness to reverberate."[2] This apparent rawness, however, is not synonymous with simplicity. As such, this crudity does not lie in a physical materiality but in the way it is manipulated to convey a sense of austerity, of highly elaborated formal nudity. The desire for abstraction that prevails in the project fails in that precise aspiration. Suppose we understand abstraction as the process through which one seeks to define generic frameworks rather than specific solutions. In that case, the house does not transcend its character as a singular work. Instead of offering a universally replicable solution, it is a profoundly individual artifact.

Critics have also described Casa Luna as an audacious and daring experiment. Any risk, however, is a fiction when played outside the rules of the game in which an architectural commission usually unfolds. Without friction, what is at stake is only one's resources. When the client and architect are one in the same,[3] the project becomes a manifesto on what architecture can be when freed from external constraints. This possibility may occasionally be virtuous, but it is undoubtedly rare for architecture: without constraints, the discipline introspectively explores a delicately drawn (and fragilely constructed) autonomy. Although Casa Luna could discuss the formal, material, and aesthetic possibilities of architecture, it remains silent when it comes to dialogue with its context – both material and rhetorical. The house is hardly replicable, and thus lifeless. Casa Luna's media success is due to the fact that the architects do not operate in the Chilean game but on a global playing field. They fulfill the

Elemental, Quinta Monroy, Iquique, Chile, 2003. Top: Quinta Monroy with informal additions, photographed in 2018. © Cristóbal Palma/Estudio Palma.

image of an end-of-the-world landscape, a fiction whose peers are not local but much farther away, in international magazines and other architecture platforms.

Outside

The "outward impulse" refers to architecture pushing against its disciplinary edges. These practices justify themselves in the measure of other (more significant) causes: from social heroism to cultural vindications of different kinds and environmental activism. If biennials, publications, and exhibitions were led by projects that focused on poverty, immigration, social injustice, and decolonialism, the most recent ones are dominated by responses to the climate and environmental crises and the rhetoric of caring for the planet. With the heroic narratives of the 20th century exhausted, altruistic causes now swing the pendulum from the discourse of social, political, and cultural responsibility to the ecological turn.

At one Machiavellian extreme is the practice in which "the end justifies the means": the commission, its context, its real social impact, or its financing do not matter because the end – the building, the architecture, the work as personal expression – is what is relevant. At the other is the architecture of means over ends (following Giorgio Agamben's *Means without Ends*). The superimposition of means and the relativization of ends bring architecture face to face with its failures of conscience and consequence, visible in participatory processes, environmental regulations and certifications, and the possibility of social impact at a territorial scale. As part of this rhetorical substitution, architecture empties itself to promote a discipline measured only by how it responds to a socially virtuous mode of practice (social participation, asking "the right question," and "political correctness" of the work), and not by the aesthetic or formal results.

Pritzker Prize–laureate Alejandro Aravena, with his firm Elemental, has been a key figure in this "movement outward," with an internationally recognized practice that showcases the local tradition of progressive and incremental housing. Through emblematic projects such as the 2003 Quinta Monroy in Iquique, Chile, he revived the international architecture agenda by emphasizing public concern and social responsibility. However, parallel to local neighborhood and housing projects, Elemental has developed a rich portfolio of global megaprojects, from Dubai to Basel and Lisbon. In their agenda for the "just city" and the state's rules for access to housing, Elemental attempts to bring together

Elemental, Energia de Portugal (edp) Headquarters, Lisbon, 2024. Photo: Francisco Nogueira.

two worlds that rarely meet in Aravena's own work: gestural explorations with an architecture that serves social utility. What this sort of practice ultimately succeeded in advancing was the ambition of a younger generation to develop a similar bipolar practice. Lack of social commitment was understood as unforgivable for the young architect, but total dedication to this kind of heroism constituted an equally naive position. The solution was to have one foot on each side, as an irreparable fracture: a good architecture or a good architect, never fully both. Aravena's double practice encapsulates the disciplinary contradiction that this essay is exposing. On the one hand, that architecture has served the elites related to power and capital. On the other, that architecture is an epistemological and political field, a public matter, and a problem, with or without buildings.

This dispute is at the heart of the work of contemporary Chilean architects, but it has deeper roots. In *De re aedificatoria*, Vitruvius already theorized that architecture is both *fabricatio* and *ratiocinatio*. In 1805, J.N.L. Durand insisted on this dialectic (and contradiction) in his *Précis*: "It is evident that pleasure can never have been the aim of architecture, nor can architectural decoration have been its object. Public and private utility, the happiness and the protection of individuals and of society: such is the aim of architecture. Whether it be accorded or denied the name of art, it will nonetheless deserve to be practiced, and the means to its end will deserve to be examined; and this we shall now do."[4]

4. J.N.L. Durand, *Précis of the Lectures on Architecture: With, the Graphic Portion of the Lectures on Architecture*, trans. David Britt (Los Angeles: Getty Research Institute, 2000), 23.

Both disciplinary autonomy and service to society were aspirations of architecture when it was first institutionalized and taught at the École des Beaux-Arts in Paris. More than a century later, Theodor Adorno, in his essay "Functionalism Today," exposed the paradox between formal autonomy and functionalism lodged in the very heart of the modernist project. Adorno criticizes functionalist statements and commitments as mere style, calling for architecture to not forget its social function. He divides the purposeful arts from the purposeless arts, which, for him, can never be absolutely separated but must coexist in a dialectical relationship.

Between objects of use and objects of art, local architecture seems placed on irreconcilable paths: those who defend inward architecture as the strict design of buildings (and good buildings usually appear hand in hand with direct commissions and economic freedom) or those who push it outward and decentralize it toward external agendas. In these antagonistic impulses, some works have shifted the compass

Smiljan Radic and Nicolás Schmidt, National Pavilion for the XXII Biennial of Architecture and Urbanism of Chile, Plaza de la Cultura, Santiago, 2023. © Cristóbal Palma/Estudio Palma.

of architecture. This is the case with the pavilion designed by Smiljan Radic and Nicolás Schmidt at the Chilean Biennial of Architecture and Urbanism in 2023.

In and Out

Installed in the square in front of La Moneda Palace in the center of Santiago, the inflatable pavilion stood for only 10 days and received about 300 visitors per day. The fragility and temporality of the inflatable structure operated in radical contrast to the solid monumentality of the government building. The sort of metallic pillow – light, improbable, and alien – seemed to float, interrupting the axis of the Pasco Bulnes. In its brief existence, this 82-by-115-foot installation was the site of open lectures and debates.

The social outrage in Chile that developed in 2018 (interrupted by the pandemic) was the largest and strongest seen in decades. From feminist protests to riots to demands for environmental, political, and cultural changes, it was as massive as it was broad in terms of its concerns and causes, and the material consequences in the city still lasts. These demonstrations and movements occurred in the city center, close to where the pavilion was installed. Its program and role standing there, in front of the government palace, was in friction with the context in many ways. Hundreds of visitors found the trust needed to enter and use this uncanny

Above and opposite page: The pavilion was built with strips of Mylar connected with transparent tape. Use of the pavilion proved that it was a "live" architectural experiment. © Cristóbal Palma/Estudio Palma.

pavilion that looked fragile and unstable. Their confidence was gained through a chain of implicit safety signals to the public: from the architects' credibility to the Colegio de Arquitectos as a client to the financial support of the Ministry of Culture. Despite this chain of trust, this was still a truly risky, potentially hazardous project, given the technical and political considerations.

The pavilion was built without a plan, drawings, or models. Mylar strips were unspooled from 4-by-164-foot rolls in a shed outside the city to test how to assemble and inflate the pillow. The main challenge was how to overlap each Mylar strip with the next. After various experiments, 25 bands were eventually connected with 6-inch transparent tape, which allowed for transparency between strips, creating both an inner luminosity and structural flexibility. In situ, however, hazards only multiplied. The structure could not sit directly on the rough concrete pavement, so wood boards had to be placed before installation could start. Once the pillow was installed and inflated, anything could become a threat to the lightweight volume, from a heeled shoe to a strong wind. Constantly assessed weights were attached to the balloon in order to keep it on the ground. One day a rioter threw a stone, puncturing the pavilion, and it started to deflate. These proved that the pavilion was a live architectural experiment that had to follow the health and safety regulations of a regular public building without any of the traditional conditions of firmness associated with building codes.

The movement embodied by the pavilion could be understood as centrifugal. It is part of Radic's long quest to research and develop pneumatic structures. However, the structure in front of La Moneda managed to be loquacious (the pavilion's fragility in the midst of that context was eloquent), and its disciplinary autonomy, resistant (it worked within the rules of the discipline however having an impact beyond itself). This duality assumed a productive form of resistance because it opens possibilities for the discipline and communicates to the larger public. The fragile pillow in the middle of a damaged city center was a powerful image. The work is an architecture that turns inward to move outward and, in so doing, finds another sensibility and engagement with the world, fleeing easy militancy or heroism. In the introduction to *El Croquis* 167 on Radic, Alejandro G. Crispiani discusses how his architecture moves freely between contradictions without definitively taking sides with any extremes. The pavilion pulls inward but without a sterile effect such as that of Casa Luna.

Such a pendulum in the Chilean panorama of work might be desired, but it is not productive at the extremes, whether in or out. At one extreme there are architectures without context (but in the pristine landscape) that explore their own formal rules and material possibilities. At the other are architectures that serve the social, the environmental, or the political with little focus on the architectural qualities of the work. In a second reading of this dialectic, "outward" refers to working from within architecture toward its edges: this implies recognition of an expanded field, beyond building. Over the quests to justify buildings between their *means* and *ends*, over the debate between architecture as an art or as social science, the urge for friction has pushed architects of my generation into this expanded field of practice, which architecture has been forced to embrace. This includes the editorial and curatorial fields, public policy, object design, the urban and landscape realms, research and academia as political and intellectual projects, and so on. The work of contemporary Chilean architects is as fertile today in this expanded field as in designing buildings.

When the possibility of an "inward" architecture becomes rare, practices have expanded to the edges of an improbable nature, like Radic's pavilion. "In and out" implies conceptualizing architecture as a defined techné with its own language and parameters and rooted in the building site, as well as understanding that architecture is an expanded field of knowledge beyond the building. Buildings, works, and their architects (*fabrica*) are never independent of a critical and collective debate that brings together both the reproductive and the productive roles (*ratiocinatio*).

A couple of generations have already produced bodies of work that have had local and foreign impact, as seen in the latest monographs on Chile. But there is some space left to question the work of contemporary Chilean architects if the discipline is understood as both a design project and a field of knowledge. What ties together the published contributions of contemporary practices is a collective rather than authorial consciousness and an attempt to build an expanded field around architecture. After five years of strong political and social change in Chile – and the world – it is worth continuing the conversations on the inward-outward impulse that has defined the local architectural debate. As social upheavals, failed constitutional trials, and the pandemic begin to settle, it is time to assess how much of the discipline was destabilized.

The dissent and division between these two movements in architecture is necessary: it is part of the critical dichotomy that allows architects and critics to redefine, deepen, and broaden architecture's limits. By so vehemently defending either the disciplinary boundaries or the expanded functions of architecture, we risk shrinking, squeezing inward, and losing sight of architecture as a thick and broadened cultural field. Furthermore, "practice" must not be immediately understood as the opposite of "theory." As Gilles Deleuze said in conversation with Michel Foucault, "Practice is a set of relays from one theoretical point to another, and theory is a relay from one practice to another."[5] In and out, practice and theory are inseparable. Embracing friction over fiction implies the exploration of dialectical modes of practice. Neither inside nor outside, interstices might be the contemporary place for the discipline.

5. Leonard Lawlor and John Nale, eds., *The Cambridge Foucault Lexicon* (Cambridge: Cambridge University Press, 2014).

Alejandra Celedón is dean at the Facultad de Arquitectura, Arte y Diseño at the Universidad Diego Portales, Chile. She curated the Chilean Pavilion's "Stadium: a building that renders the image of a city" at the 2018 Venice Architecture Biennale, and she directs the archival project "Santiago *Microcosmos*."

Carlos Eduardo Binato de Castro
& Suelen Camerin

Inhabiting
The Landscape

From 1979 to 1981, Miguel Eyquem Astorga designed and built Casa en Portezuelo in Colina, Chile, for his friend Luis Peña. In 2010–12, Smiljan Radic designed and built Casa para el Poema del Ángulo Recto in Vilches, Chile, for his family. Eyquem was a pilot, an architect, an urban planner, and a professor at the School of Architecture at the Catholic University of Valparaíso. In addition to participating in creating the Ciudad Abierta of Ritoque, Chile, in 1972, throughout his career Eyquem produced diverse architectural projects, including single-family houses, urban plans, and institutional work. He died in 2021, age 98. Radic graduated from the Pontifical Catholic University of Chile in Santiago in 1989, and in 1995 opened a practice that was soon acclaimed for works of unquestionable quality, materially diverse, with complex geometry and unusual forms. Radic is recognized for the extensive and varied references that inform his architectural imaginary, including literature, theater, sculpture, illustration, collage, and everyday objects.

In a 2014 article titled "Some Remains of My Heroes Found Scattered in a Vacant Lot,"[1] Radic mentions Eyquem's house in Portezuelo. Among the texts, photographs, sketches, and collages that illustrate the article, there are three photographs of the house, which Radic renames "Casa de los Bichos," or House of Bugs. He writes that the images "illustrate the abandoned routine that overflows every corner of that Chilean house, enveloped in a strange and memorable penumbra: fossilized bugs, dried bugs, bugs displayed in glass cases, live bugs…, turtles, hawks, flies, iguanas…, boxes full of dead niches, bones and scientific names…, then the man, the arrows and the blankets."[2] The photographs show shelves full of boxes from Peña's collection, the renowned entomologist on a chair in the hallway, seen from the upper part of the patio close to the undulating ceiling, and a panoramic view of the entire house seen from the entrance. The last image seems to arouse special interest, as Radic draws attention to the "living ivy hanging from the sky as if, by stubborn nature, it were taking its place again – the one that was expropriated from it by construction – now classified by a scientifically

1. This article is the transcription of a lecture given by Radic at the seminar "La luna de acuerdo…," organized by the Master in Architecture of the Pontifical Catholic University of Chile in May 2014. See Smiljan Radic, "Algunos restos de mis héroes encontrados dispersos en un sitio baldío," *ARQ+2: Smiljan Radic Bestiario*, (2014): 52.
2. Radic, "Algunos restos de mis heroes," 52. Our translation.
3. Ibid.

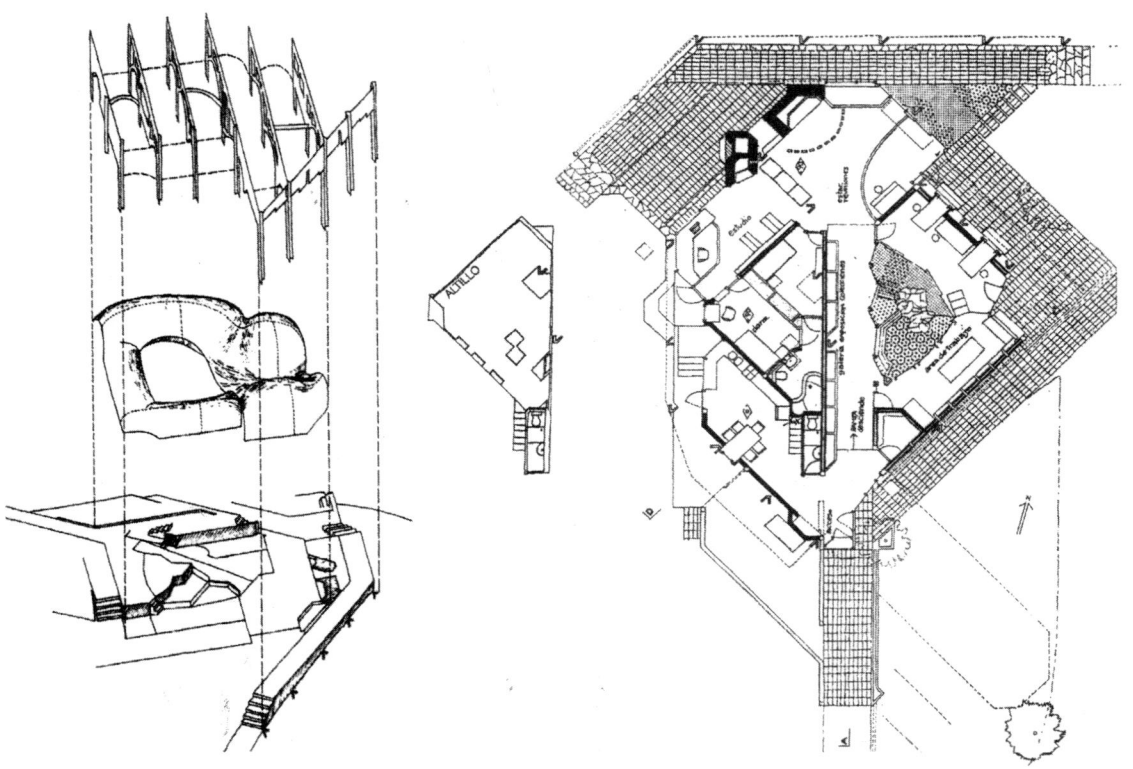

Miguel Eyquem Astorga, Casa en Portezuelo, Colina, Chile, 1981. Left: Exploded isometric drawing detailing the structure. Right: Plan drawing of the house with the entry toward the bottom of the drawing, the living quarters to the left, the institute rooms to the right and the living room at the top. Drawings courtesy Archivo Histórico José Vial Armstrong, Escuela de Arquitectura y Diseño, PUCV.

everyday disorder, filling its walls up to the sky curved in a cave, or a cemetery crammed with names."[3]

Eyquem in Portezuelo

The Casa en Portezuelo is a reflection of Eyquem's multi-disciplinary training: it articulates the architect's spatial thinking, the urban planner's perception of the landscape, and the pilot's aerodynamic knowledge. The 250-square-meter house is both the researcher's residence and the headquarters of the Juan Ignacio Molina Institute. It is located on a small hill next to Los Libertadores highway, which connects Santiago to Colina. The structure of the house is entirely constructed of reinforced concrete, cast on site. Six narrow beams of different shapes and depths rest on slender pillars and support a thin roof that undulates according to the distribution of the spaces below. The floor adapts to the topographical variations of the terrain, and the internal spaces are cooled by the constant movement of breezes through the difference in levels between the concrete slab and the metal roof. Wrapping around the internal spaces is a balcony that both shades the glass facades and serves as an

Casa en Portezuelo, still from "In Lieblicher Bläue/En el amable azul: Conversaciones con Miguel Eyquem," 2020. Courtesy Archivo Histórico José Vial Armstrong, Escuela de Arquitectura y Diseño, PUCV.

observation deck to overlook the surrounding landscape.

The plan is essentially square, rotated 45 degrees such that the main entrance axis is from one corner. The central corridor cuts the house in half diagonally and leads to the living room, located at the opposite end. To the left of the entrance are the kitchen, bedrooms, bathrooms, and Peña's office; to the east, around an internal courtyard, are the rooms that house the institute. The house is more introspective toward the south, with opaque mid-height walls, and more open in the other directions, with balconies and glass enclosures.

Despite the seemingly complex layout of the spaces, most of the rooms are square or rectangular in plan. The institute space holds the shelves and cabinets that store the insects Peña collected and cataloged during his travels throughout South America. Peña also has a private office adjacent to the living room and a small workstation in a loft space above the bedrooms, which takes advantage of the high ceilings at the center of the house.

The house was built with a limited budget – the funds were from the sale of a small house in Santia – and with limited labor: Peña, Eyquem, three interns, a carpenter, a

Casa en Portezuelo, still from "In Lieblicher Bläue." A view from the north side of the house where concrete shades span between columns. Courtesy Archivo Histórico José Vial Armstrong, Escuela de Arquitectura y Diseño, PUCV.

bricklayer, a plumber, and an electrician.[4] The structural system of perforated beams, pillars, and undulating slabs was designed to reduce the amount of material used and, consequently, the final weight of the structure, as well as to guarantee the free flow of air.[5] It is almost as if the structure were metal and the concrete fulfilled the function of cladding and covering: "It is an iron beam, but made of concrete," according to Eyquem.[6]

The palette of materials, all raw, is minimal. The interior floors are smooth, slightly shiny concrete, and the exterior ones are cut rectangles of stone with a rough texture. Raw stone also covers the walls of the chimneys and the retaining walls surrounding the house. Red ceramic brick, which forms the interior and exterior walls, was laid in full joint, vertically, horizontally, or rotated at 45 degrees, always without stucco but sometimes painted white. The reinforced concrete shapes all the structural elements and has varied textures. The pillars and beams register the narrow wood planks of the formwork and the slabs, the rectangular sheets of flexible plywood. Externally, the concrete slabs did not receive any finish; inside, they were painted white. The glass that encloses the house is trimmed with conventional wood or metal frames, the corrugated tiles covering the concrete elements are metal, and the solar protection elements in the west gallery are made of wood.

4. Miguel Eyquem, *Hormigón en obra. Forma resistente 6.1. Eyquem + Jolly, Baixas + del Río, Izquierdo + Lehmann, Radic + Correa* (Santiago: Ediciones ARQ, 2009), 30.
5. Ibid.
6. "In Lieblicher Bläue/En el amable azul: Conversaciones con Miguel Eyquem." 2020, posted August 30, 2021, by Dereojo Comunicaciones, Vimeo, 1 hour, 24 minutes, https://vimeo.com/ondemand/enelamableazul.
7. "Smiljan Radic: Gravedad y algo de Gracia," lecture, July 17, 2020, RCR Bunka Fundació Privada, YouTube, 1 hour, 33 minutes, https://www.youtube.com/watch?v=F3SIiNDVKhY&t=952s.
8. Moises Puente, "Almost Eight Hectares," *Apartamento*, 12 (2013-14): 121.
9. Ibid.

Casa en Portezuelo, still from "In Lieblicher Bläue." Inside, concrete walls and glass partitions stop short of the undulating ceiling. Cutouts in the ceiling expose the beams and the metal roof as well as allow light and air into the rooms. Courtesy Archivo Histórico José Vial Armstrong, Escuela de Arquitectura y Diseño, PUCV.

Radic in Vilches

The Casa para el Poema del Ángulo Recto is Radic's version of Oscar Wilde's castle of the selfish giant.[7] In the tale, the giant, returning from a seven-year absence, finds his castle garden invaded by children. He immediately builds a very high wall around it and puts up a no trespassing sign to scare away visitors. Perpetual winter settles on the garden. The giant is puzzled. Where was spring? Only when the children return through a hole in the wall does the garden bloom again, and the giant, recognizing his error, tears the wall down.

In response to the possible form of the castle, in 2010, Radic created a model that would resolve the public-private relationship raised in the tale. The volume – a semi-perforated torus with appendages that could form supports or skylights – becomes the home of his own family. This "castle" is on the edge of a hill in Vilches. The rural plot belongs to Radic and his wife, the sculptor Marcela Correa, whose family has owned the property since the 1970s. Radic and Correa acquired the land in the 1990s, and over the years added to it as they constructed other buildings, including Casa Chica, a small house built in 1995 and later transformed into a swimming pool around 2010;[8] Casa A, a wood chalet renovated in 2007 and destroyed by the 2010 earthquake, Casa Transparente and Cabana de Heidegger, two houses that were renovated and incorporated into the complex with the acquisition of neighboring lots;[9] and finally, Atelie Corral, a

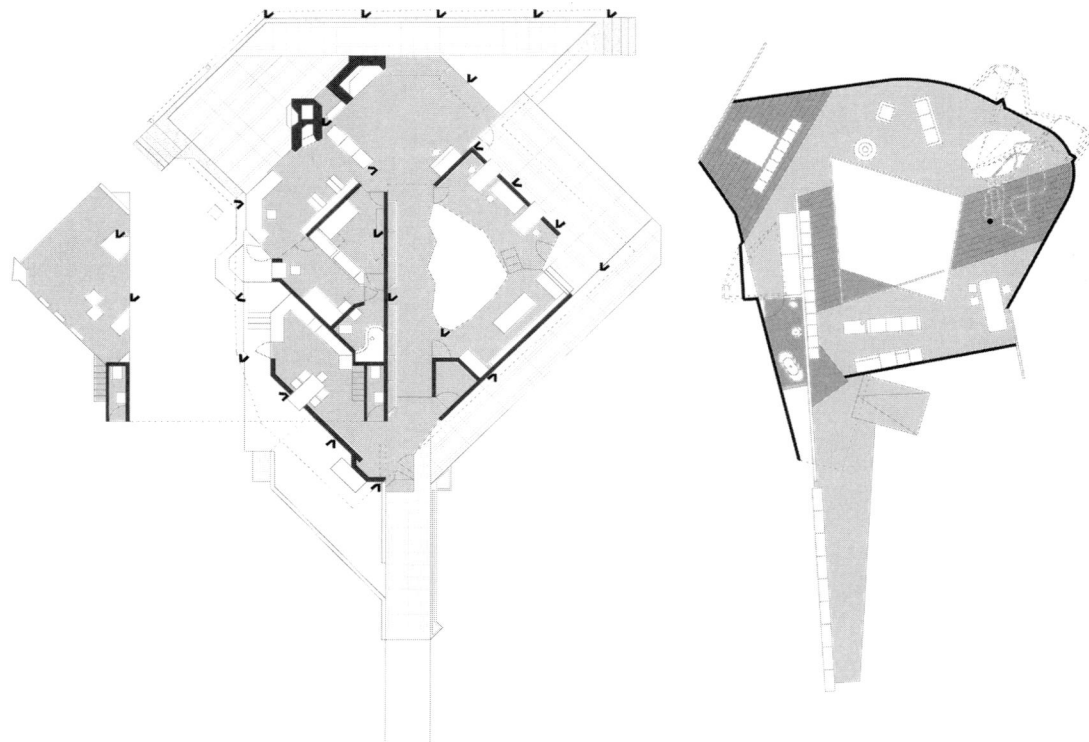

Left: Casa en Portezuelo. Right: Smiljan Radic, Casa para el Poema del Ángulo Recto, Vilches, Chile, 2012. Plans redrawn by the authors.

space that houses Correa's sculptures, built in 2015.

Despite Radic's reference to Wilde's story, the name of the house refers to *The Poem of the Right Angle* painting series by Le Corbusier from 1947 to '53. Radic says he sought to re-create the cavernous feeling depicted in painting C.2 for the internal atmosphere of his house.[10] In this painting, a man is lying down and a woman is crouching in a kind of cave, formed by the space under a large hand; in the background, the sky appears in an amoeboid opening. Among the rooms of Radic's house, the one that most faithfully reproduces this atmosphere is the main bedroom, which has low ceilings and a double bed in the center, facing a square window that frames a view of the landscape.

The house is a single space, opaque on the outside and transparent on the inside. The activities surround a glassed-in garden – essentially an open-plan courtyard house – that is enclosed in an irregular perimeter of black-painted concrete. Access is via a long, disproportionate platform – an over-extended tongue[11] – with a short ramp close to the entry. The interior is not compartmentalized; each function has its place but the floating furniture gives the opposite impression. The route through the gallery that surrounds the courtyard begins

10. Radic, "Gravedad y algo de Gracia."
11. Alejandro G. Crispiani, "El juego de los contrarios," *El Croquis* 167 (2013): 32.

Casa para el Poema del Ángulo Recto. The exterior from the north side, with multi-angled skylights over the living room. © Cristóbal Palma/Estudio Palma.

in the kitchen, passes through the dining corner, continues through the living room and bedrooms, and ends in the wardrobe space.

The structure of the house is a 12-centimeter-thick reinforced-concrete shell. The maximum span is 15 meters; one isolated white cylindrical pillar is camouflaged among Correa's sculptures. In addition to the central garden, the house opens up to the landscape at other strategic points without losing the exterior opacity: at the entrance, at the windows of the dining area, in the bedroom and the bathroom. In addition, there are three skylights in the form of a faceted conical trunk, two over the living room and one over the children's bedroom. The windows are planes that slide on exterior rails, independent of the walls of the sculptural volume, its black shell helping to camouflage the prism in the surrounding forest. The interior is clad with cedar and

Casa para el Poem del Ángulo Recto. The west side of the house, showing the main bedroom window and the skylight over the children's bedroom. Opposite page: A view from the main bedroom looking toward the living room (left) and into the courtyard. © Cristóbal Palma/Estudio Palma.

white-painted plaster. From the outside, the house is rough, opaque, uncomfortable, and strange; inside, it is smooth, shiny, cozy, and familiar.

Inhabiting the Landscape

The apparent formal distinctions between Eyquem's house and Radic's house can mask their less obvious similarities. The massive presence of cast-in-place concrete as a structural material is perhaps the most obvious. In both houses, concrete shapes the elements that stand out for their slenderness: pillars, beams, and undulating roof in Portezuelo and the faceted wall-ceiling in Vilches. And the plans of the two houses revolve around irregularly shaped glazed central courtyards. Other than that, the houses seem to be opposites: while Eyquem's is extroverted and has a transparent periphery, Radic's is introspective and has an opaque envelope. When Eyquem uses pillars, beams, and slabs to create a composition of planes, Radic uses load-bearing walls that become roof slabs in a composition of volumes. In Portezuelo, the house sits gently on the crest of a small hill, while in Vilches, it cantelivers over a slope; Eyquem's house is an undulating white roof that covers, while Radic's is a black wall that embraces.

The strongest connection between the two houses seems to be the influence of their sites on their designs. Nature shapes Eyquem's project beyond aerodynamics and its ability to cool everything beneath the undulating slab. Eyquem's drawings that emphasize the presence of the El Plomo and La Campana hills show his concern for relating to nature beyond the house's lot. The domestic environment flows out to the surrounding balconies and also serves as shelter in the middle of the natural immensity around the house. The interior plateaus of the rooms were also adapted to the natural topography, with the intention to leave nature almost intact.

The strong interiority of Radic's project, evidenced by the apparent denial of the exterior, is reinforced by the arrangement of the internal spaces around the sexagenarian tree in the center of the courtyard. From inside the house, the view outward is upward, toward the sky, with no apparent horizon line. The boundary between interior and exterior dissolves in the interior garden, which merges with the objects and furniture that populate the house. Although closing off the exterior may seem odd, given the exuberance of the surrounding nature, Radic says that the inhabitants of the house are so familiar with the landscape that they

12. Smiljan Radic, "Casa para el Poema del Ángulo Recto," *El Croquis* 167: 224.

recognize it by its signs and sounds, without needing to look directly at it all the time.[12]

Eyquem and Radic designed different artifacts for different environments. Eyquem finds a rural setting in an arid landscape, 30 kilometers north of Santiago, with sparse vegetation, dry land, small dispersed trees, and a scattered surrounding, where the divergent gaze expands and pushes out horizontally. Radic finds a rural setting in a humid landscape, 300 kilometers south of Santiago, with dense vegetation, dry leaves, medium-sized trees, and an introverted surrounding, where the convergent gaze escapes vertically. In Portezuelo, Eyquem's architecture is more plane than volume, more roof than wall, as straight as it is curved, as compartmentalized as it is open. It is transparent right where the weight levitates in the air – it is almost a hut. In Vilches, Radic's architecture is more volume than plane, more wall than roof, as curved as it is straight, as open as it is compartmentalized, it is opaque right where the weight rests on the ground – it is almost a cave. Each masterfully inhabits the surrounding landscape in its particular way.

Carlos Eduardo Binato de Castro is a PhD student in history, theory, and criticism of architecture at the Universidade Federal do Rio Grande do Sul (UFRGS) Research and Postgraduate Program in Architecture, Brazil (PROPAR). Suelen Camerin received a PhD from PROPAR in 2022 and is now a professor in the Department of Architecture, UFRGS.

Florencia Rodríguez
with Jaime Solares Carmona

Criticism And Dispersion

Florencia Rodríguez is an architect, writer, editor, and lecturer, and, since 2022, the director of the School of Architecture at the University of Illinois Chicago. A Loeb Fellow at the Harvard Graduate School of Design in 2013–14, Rodríguez cofounded the magazine PLOT *in 2010, which she directed until 2017, when she became founding editorial director of Lots of Architecture and the magazine* –NESS. *She has taught at the School of Architecture of Universidad Torcuato Di Tella and Universidad de Palermo, both in Argentina, the Universidad Nacional del Litoral, Tecnológico de Monterrey, Harvard, and the Boston Architectural College. She was recently appointed the artistic director of the 2025 Chicago Architecture Biennial. Our conversation took place over Zoom on September 30, 2024. – JSC*

JAIME SOLARES: How do you think your work as a professor, editor, curator, critic, and researcher feed into each other, and what can criticism do that these other activities cannot?

FLORENCIA RODRÍGUEZ: For a long time, I have tried to develop some definitions for practicing critical activism or active criticism, but I think that what defines me better is that I am a cultural producer, and as such, I put together different formats and media. I believe that architecture is a cultural practice, and there are various forms or vehicles I can adopt, like teaching, curating, or publishing. At the end of the day, what I'm trying to do is to facilitate collective encounters where we can think critically about contemporary narratives and interpret what we are doing and how we impact our built environment. You will notice that I prefer to use the word *narrative* instead of *discourse*. That is because it better responds to the multiplicity and pluralism of the array of different intellectual expressions. All the different formats I was alluding to can activate or participate in organizing new debates and conversations. Of course, putting together a pedagogical project is very different from what one expects in a publication, for example. But the scope of my work as a critic is more related to cultural production in architecture and to understanding how you generate different outcomes in those specific venues or formats.

PLOT 24: América Latina Hoy (April/May 2015). Rodríguez was the editorial director of *PLOT* from its launch in 2010 to 2017.

JS: Would it be fair to say that instead of criticism sensu stricto, you are more concerned with critical thinking in cultural production?

FR: I would agree with that. We can ask what criticism is nowadays or what the formats or the vehicles for the dissemination and evolution of ideas are today. I am interested in criticism in general and in our current cultural situation. I feel there is the urge for original ideas and the creation of new concepts.

JS: As you said, you can be a critic activist or an activist who thinks critically. Either way, you are always very optimistic about the possibilities of architecture. In that sense, what is this concept of "revoluciones discretas," or "discreet revolutions"? A revolution toward what?

FR: I am probably a pathological optimist. I believe architecture is an optimistic discipline because we are projecting ideas for possible futures and speculating about the impacts that may arise from them. I don't feel alone in that optimism, even though there is a strong critical tradition that operates in the opposite way.

Words, images, objects have the power to generate territories (or cultural fields) and facilitate all sorts of collective endeavors. Starting a conversation, whether in a class, through an article, or at a conference – or even certain decisions when projecting a building or a public space – can be transformative and impact one person or a small group. That's what I mean by discreet revolutions. These transformations are not necessarily huge or immediately radical but then there is the organic evolution of ideas, the dispersion.

But I like the part of your question about the revolution's direction. We constantly hear that we need to make an impact and the meaning of that impact becomes either emptied or too heavy of a load. Making an impact is permanent, and it could also have negative connotations, so what kind of impact makes a difference? We need to start being more specific and intentional. The potential to change can start small but it requires care and engagement.

One of the small things I have enjoyed most about my work is putting together two people who don't know each other in a publication or on a panel discussion and then seeing how they continue the conversation or collaborate afterward. The scale of this change is not big but reduced and interpersonal. I am not changing the direction of the field, but I am facilitating a collaboration that positions specific ideas or an agenda. I take very seriously the responsibility of writing, teaching, or directing a school. That's why I like the concept of discreet revolutions. When you scale down that ambition and understand that what you do in your small network makes a difference, it makes more sense to do it. And it's easier to find meaning.

JS: Maybe the key word to understand this concept is *network* and how it is a counterpoint to the heroism that was so important for Latin American architecture in the past.

FR: Yes, interconnectivity and the value of the collective are also related to a canonless or center-less moment. Or, as I prefer to think of it, the era of dispersion, a more plural moment without a unique canon but a multiplicity of narratives.

Universal heroic ideas usually embody one determined idea of progress toward a specific scenario, and that doesn't seem to represent who we are in the world today. I prefer to think about smaller narratives that represent specific contexts and can intertwine with other places. I also believe in the value of global communication and of learning from different idiosyncrasies, contexts, and possibilities. There's an opportunity between the small and the big, the singular and the international situation. I think that's a more fertile territory now than thinking about universal discourses.

But this clearly doesn't come without resistance. When we look at global politics today, we are torn by these polarized, canonical extremes that are for sure not representing an understanding of our world today.

JS: You work with this idea of "criticism in the age of dispersion." What do you mean by that?

FR: As in politics, there is a lot of nostalgia for clear canons or universal ideas in architecture. I see a recurrent tension between autonomy and engagement – the discipline from within, with its own independent set of rules, versus how we interpret its relationships to the world. Put simply, many people still believe that we, as designers, lose agency when architecture responds to its social context or to very specific situations, and question what is left of the discipline. I

-*NESS.docs* 2: Landscape as Urbanism in the Americas (2020). -*NESS* is published by Lots of Architecture, which was cofounded by Rodríguez in 2017.

believe that controversy shouldn't exist. The prejudice might be based on some aspects of the golden years of theory and criticism in architecture, and probably some misreading of poststructuralism or other very strong and exciting intellectual trends that, in some circles, became operative and endogamous. But things seem to be changing.

The idea of dispersion defines our time, but it is not new. We could go back to Foucault, who in 1978, in a lecture at the French Society of Philosophy called "What is Critique?," defined critique as something inevitably, and by nature, "condemned to dispersion, dependency and pure heteronomy." The new vehicles and means of criticism emphasize, even more, those conditions. Social media has only helped in the exponential growth of voices sharing opinions everywhere, which represents a magnificent opportunity for the expansion of old canons and the democratization of knowledge. But, of course, we always need to red-flag the dangers of intellectual echo chambers, which are also part of this phenomenon.

Dispersion is part of the nature of discourse. That's why I'm interested in the idea of territory, field, or the mechanics of gossip. You start talking to somebody, and as it evolves, the conversation continues to grow and opens to other interlocutors. What is interesting about dispersion is the lack of control over the narrative. You put ideas out there, and then they evolve collectively. This challenges any idea of progress as a preset direction.

JS: Thinking of dispersion alongside dissolution might be helpful in this case. Dissolution helps us understand the territorial dimension of this spreading. Given our era of the image, television, mass communication, etc., and how ideas get stretched and flattened, how does dispersion affect the depth of the discussion?

FR: The discussion on social media is probably not always that deep, but I think it has the power to affect culture as it socializes and installs certain issues or intellectual trends.

Another complex aspect of this is the velocity at which it all happens. You mentioned the flattening, which is something you can see clearly with younger generations that are digital natives. Many tend to flatten history and all sorts of ideas without being able to organize them chronologically or conceptually, which represents a big pedagogical challenge. That's why it is important to understand the editorial and curatorial practices as critical activities that can organize conceptual constellations – as I have liked to call them since *PLOT*. Some kind of meaning emerges from that.

JS: One of *PLOT*'s main objectives is to foster a broader exchange between Argentine, Latin American, and global discussions. Almost 15 years later, what has changed in this relationship, especially concerning the United States?

FR: *PLOT* was conceived as a response to what I understood as a vacant space in its context. Its project was inscribed in a tradition of publications that, like *Domus* or *Casabella*, put together theory, criticism, industry, and practice.

When we started the magazine, my main intellectual project was to feature Latin American production while pairing it with other global and well-known practices. I thought, and still think, that a lot of the architecture that is now being produced in Latin America has an outstanding quality and specific value for our current times. However, we often lack narratives or discourses to interpret those architectures. More textual and intellectual work is produced in the North while more architecture from emerging practices is built in the South. This is related particularly to the processes that mediate architectural production in both places. In the North, there are more regulations and constraints, more consultants, and a more deterministic real estate market. In the South, regulations are softer, there is room to respond to more immediate needs, and even for certain improvisation or "ad hocism." Some things are solved on the construction site, and the architect has much more agency.

This phenomenon affects each country differently. Latin America is not a homogeneous territory, but we share historical processes such as colonization and modernization, and how they relate to the birth of our countries. In Latin America, production demands that the architect have a greater knowledge of construction. There is a different pathos from that in the North, which affects what the architect can do here and there.

Young practices in Latin America have more possibilities to build something, whereas, in the US, it is challenging for a young practice to build something in a city and to be part of that conversation. At the same time, academia, grants, and cultural systems that allow you to think and generate a specific theory around your practice exist much more in the North than in the South. In the South, you don't have the resources for that. That makes for an interesting conversation when you put people from both places around the table. It creates a productive reciprocity that brings different aspects of the discipline to such a challenging moment.

JS: There is a region that is rich in theoretical thinking – I call it the Pampas, but it could also be the Rioplatense region – which encompasses Argentina, Uruguay, and the south of Brazil. This theoretical thinking includes names such as Jorge Francisco (Pancho) Liernur, Marina Waisman, Carlos Eduardo Comas, Edson da Cunha Mahfuz, the group La Escuelita, founded by Rafael Viñoly and Antonio Diaz, etc. Why do you think this region has such a strong theoretical and critical tradition?

FR: Many things contributed to this phenomenon. One was the political situation in Argentina during the dictatorship (1976–83), which led to a scenario of radical thinking from which those people would emerge. You couldn't be very active because of the political persecution, people were disappearing, but this cultivated another way of understanding the discipline that became very influential afterward. Many of those thoughts arose from a circumscribed group of people through enormous individual effort. For example, Pancho Liernur founded a way of understanding the history of architecture in Argentina and gathered a group of friends who also participated in that by writing essential texts and dissertations – Graciela Silvestri, Adrián Gorelik, Anahí Ballent, Claudia Schmidt, and Fernando Aliata, among others. Liernur also

worked with Manfredo Tafuri for a period and brought back to Argentina his way of understanding history and critical thinking inscribed in Marxist materialism. An intellectual project emerged and grew from this. Liernur also curated, with Comas, Patricio del Real, and Barry Bergdoll, the MoMA exhibition "Latin America in Construction: Architecture 1955–1980," in 2015. This was also a desire to transform the discipline.

That generation did a great job in terms of refounding and giving visibility to some different "histories" of Latin American architecture, but I think there is still a pending project related to contemporary criticism and theory, and that's where we may come into the picture. We will sometimes generate friction with these historians and other times align our ideas. Either way, we face the difficult situation of finding narratives for the present. How do we make ideas operative and productive, collectively, in that context? I have no doubt there are interesting groups of people in Argentina, Chile, Brazil, and Uruguay who are working on this now, many times expanding to other disciplines. However, our social emergencies often shift our attention to more urgent practice-related matters.

JS: I'm always fascinated by how Argentina has historically built a strong relationship with the United States and vice versa. We can cite the Anybody conference, and book, in Buenos Aires, in 1996, which the Anyone Corporation organized. On the one hand, it's a very individual effort to mobilize these discussions, but they have been going on for some time. On the other hand, I think we are still very self-centered in Brazil, both in terms of our architectural references in the design process and in the discussion of theory and criticism. You say that the success of modernism in the region cast a shadow that somehow complicates the development of theoretical discussions and new narratives. Do you think anything has changed in the last five or 10 years? Or are we still under this shadow?

FR: It is changing, though I think the shadow of modernism is still strong because of its heroic legacy, which is hard to compete with. Its production was magnificent and unique! So it's easy to understand why we are so attached to it. It represents the first moment in postcolonial history in which Latin America was an active producer of a cultural transformation at the time it was also happening in Europe and North America. Before that, during the building of republican or colonial cities in Latin America, we were still importing aesthetics and trying to copy models that were not our own, while overlapping them with the pre-Columbian and vernacular. In the first half of the 20th century, there was a very active triangle of influences between Europe, North America, and South America, in which the three vertices were equally active. We can think of Le Corbusier's famous trip to South America, in 1929, and how it was transformative as he learned from Niemeyer and others. It's interesting to read about this in Bergdoll's text for the "Latin America in Construction" exhibition. One was not simply influencing the other or imposing their own agenda, rather there was a reciprocity and mutual learning. Everybody was bringing something to the table. When you see some of the first modern public buildings in Brazil, like the Ministry of Health and Education (1936), you understand the cultural weight, the unique responses to its context, the original use of concrete, the combination of architecture, landscape, and the arts and crafts, added to the dream of a new political order. I want to honor that, but I also think we need to move past it. The world has changed, and Latin America is producing excellent architecture that is environmentally conscious without necessarily advocating only

for sustainability. Of course there is the use of local materials that consume less resources in their production and transportation, and the weather conditions usually help with passive conditioning systems. There is also the understanding of idiosyncrasies and context, but all of these factors perform without compromising the aesthetic dimension or spatial ambition. Many of the values of that contemporary Latin American architecture can be traced to the modern genealogy but now are different, and I hope we can build on that.

Architects such as Macías Peredo or Productora in Mexico, GRU.A or Gustavo Utrabo in Brazil, adamo-faiden or Estudio Planta by Ana Rascovsky in Argentina, Pezo von Ellrichshausen or Smiljan Radic in Chile, among so many others, are clearly immersed in other current discussions. New realism, the open plan and the "diffuse" in interesting typological experiments, the inside-outside relation, porosity and permeability, the contingent and the permanent, are some of the issues that are very present in their production. It's only a question of promoting the narratives and conversations about things that are already happening.

JS: We are basically saying that, in a sense, more recent production has overcome the modernist ethos through this very intuitive and pragmatic approach to architecture. It does not come from a vast theoretical discussion, like in the '70s in the US, but from practice and how it has been reinventing itself.

FR: Yes, and I don't mean to simplify the intellectual efforts of these architects. What I am saying is that the balance is different, that the context impacts in a way that they can produce more objects and fewer texts. There are intellectual projects, but they are not directly related to a textual production that conceptualizes certain ideas that can go beyond the limits of each of the practices.

JS: It's a way of practicing and thinking that comes along but is not necessarily mediated by previous theoretical thinking – a praxis from the South.

FR: But I think it's important to socialize these ideas so they can become a collective and critical project. That's why I'm interested in pushing new narratives. And my claim and advocacy are for more people to write and produce exhibitions, conferences, and other cultural outcomes to organize these ideas in a way that can be collective and part of bigger discussions. There are some allies for this in Latin America for sure. *PLOT*, *ARQ* in Chile, *Liga* and *Proyector* in Mexico, among others, have been doing amazing work.

JS: In a sense, we are back to discussing dispersion and dissolution and how we can make this knowledge, this collective practice, also collectively accessible.

FR: Exactly. Dispersion and dissolution don't mean the disappearance of added values or the impossibility of generating meaning, but on the contrary, more of a spilling, dissemination, and redistribution. It is that revolution away from a contained universal discourse and toward a collectivity, a constellation of the diverse, that I am interested in.

JS: Finally, I want to hear about your following projects. What's next?

FR: My plate is quite full right now! I'm directing the School of Architecture at UIC, where we have launched and sustained a very strong and inclusive public program, as well as a journal called *Pollen*. In my personal practice, I'm working on a couple of books and collaborating on a project for the Venice Biennale, together with Christopher Hawthorne and Johnston Marklee. But the biggest news is that I have been appointed as the artistic director of the next Chicago Architecture Biennial, which opens in September 2025!

JS: Congratulations!

FR: Thank you! I was looking for a way to continue collectively developing some of the ideas we have discussed and others, and I think the biennial timing is perfect in this sense. The title is "Shift. Architecture in Times of Radical Change."

JS: What does "Shift" mean for this project?

FR: "Shift" is responding to the great cultural transformations of our time and how they affect the field of architecture and the role of design in shaping possible futures. As a critic and educator, I strongly believe in and advocate for the capabilities of our design disciplines. I'm thinking about this biennial as collective, multilayered, and multidimensional, and responding to the ideas of dispersion and dissolution we were just discussing. I'm designing formats and open calls that can put together voices from very diverse backgrounds in a productive way. There will be podcasts, videos, streaming, a series of publications, a global school network, and other participatory platforms.

We want to build an intentional archive of the contemporary and discuss new directions that can inform thinking, pedagogies, and even policies. "Shift" wants to learn from past and current experiences, exploring not only a change in focus or direction but also redefinitions in the field's substance and fundamentals. I hope we can continue the conversation there!

Jaime Solares Carmona, guest editor of *Log* 62's section on criticism in South America, is a researcher at the Critical Thinking and Contemporary City Research Group/USP.

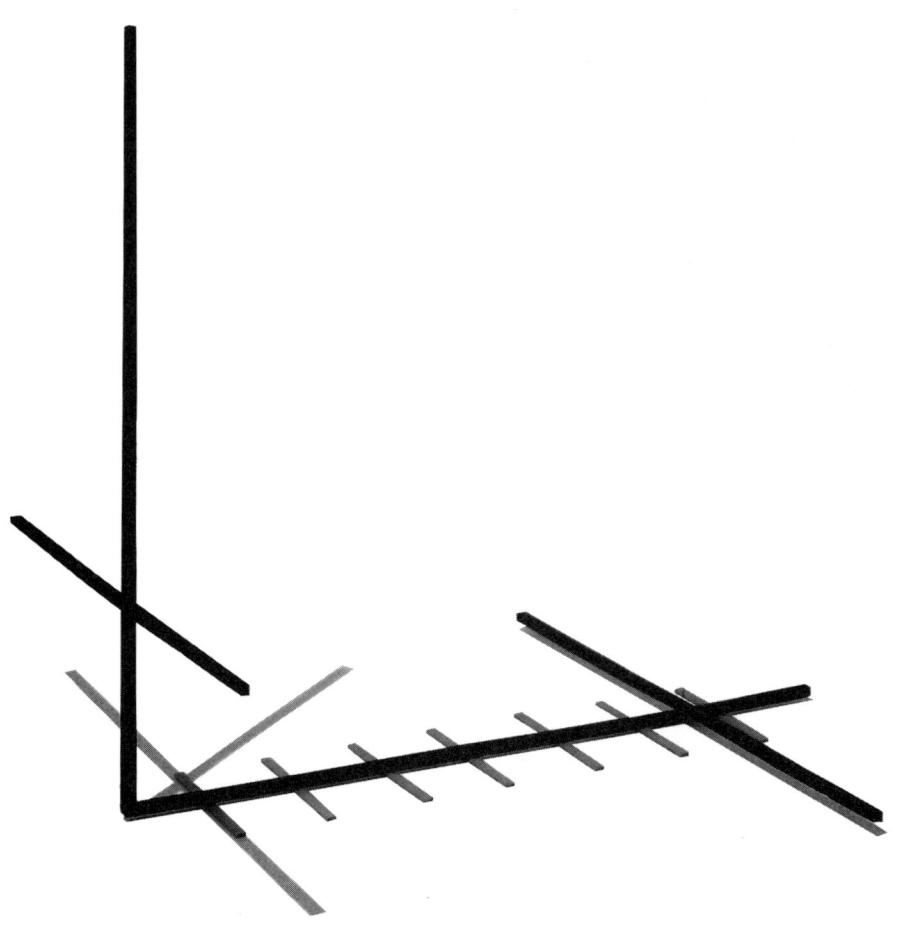

Carla Juaçaba, Vatican Chapel, Holy See Pavilion, 16th Venice Architecture
Biennale, 2018. Drawing courtesy the architect.